CHRIST
THE KING
ICON OF LOVE

RAYMOND TOMKINSON

kevin
mayhew

First published in Great Britain in 2019 by Kevin Mayhew Ltd
Buxhall, Stowmarket, Suffolk IP14 3BW
Tel: +44 (0) 1449 737978 Fax: +44 (0) 1449 737834
E-mail: info@kevinmayhew.com

www.kevinmayhew.com

9 8 7 6 5 4 3 2 1 0

ISBN 978 1 84867 979 5
Catalogue No. 1501600

Cover design by Rob Mortonson
© Image used under licence from Shutterstock Inc.
Edited by Virginia Rounding
Typeset by Angela Selfe

Printed and bound in Great Britain

Contents

About the author

Raymond Tomkinson spent some time in religious life before becoming a State Registered Nurse specialising in the care of elderly people and in hospice care. He was a hospital manager and staff development officer before training for ordained ministry. Raymond has been a parish priest and area dean in the Church of England and has also held vocations adviser and clergy development posts. He was director of a diocesan retreat centre until 2006. In 2005 he began working at Ripon College Cuddesdon, an Anglican theological college and seminary near Oxford. Following four years serving as a visiting spiritual director Raymond went on to serve for five years as College Chaplain with some teaching responsibilities in the field of Christian spirituality. In 2010 he was awarded a Master's degree in Ministry (Distinction) by Oxford Brookes University. He is an experienced spiritual director and leader of quiet days and retreats. Raymond lives in Rutland with his wife, Rose, near their daughter and her family.

Other works by Raymond Tomkinson published by Kevin Mayhew include *Come to me . . .* (2000), *God's Good Fruit* (2002), *God's Advent People* (2003), *Clothed in Christ* (2008), *Hard Time Praying?* (2009), *Life Shaping Spirituality* (2014) and *Called to Greatness: reflections on vocation and ambition in the Church* (2015).

Acknowledgements

Inspiration for this book came, initially, from conversations with the Reverend David Cowie. I am grateful for his reflections from his own devotion to Christ the King. I am grateful to the Venerable John Cox for his advice and support with early drafts of the book and to the Reverend Tom Carson for his painstaking and meticulous help with the final draft. Many thanks to the team at Kevin Mayhew Ltd, especially to Rob Mortonson for his inspired cover design. I am grateful, also, to Virginia Rounding for her patient editing of the text.

Over several decades my wife and I have joined in family celebrations at the church of Christ the King in Coventry. As guests of her sister, Josie, with her husband Jimmy and the McElroy family, we have been inspired by their faithfulness and the devotion of the clergy and congregation there.

As always, I am grateful for the support of Rose and my family who ensure I have space to think, to pray and to write.

A hymn to Christ the King[1]

Christ our King who reigns in glory,
yet who dwells so deep within;
draw us to your heart of mercy.
Hold us in Love's strong embrace.

Lord and prophet to the nations,
telling of your healing power;
show us by your death and rising,
this is now our saving hour.

Gazing now o'er all creation,
silent witness to God's love.
Arms outstretched! Inclusive welcome!
Draw us all to heaven above.

Blessed Jesus, here in Spirit,
making us a holy people;
form us as a priestly nation,
bidding us to pray in you.

Crown upon your blood-stained brow
shows the price of Kingly power;
marks a royal coronation:
triumph in that bitter hour.

---

1. May be sung to the tune of 'Come, thou long-expected Jesus' (Cross of Jesus) by
Sir John Stainer.

Wounded Healer, sore afflicted,
hands and feet and more beside;
arms outstretched in loving welcome:
hide us in your piercèd side.

Christ our King now reigns in glory
o'er all worlds in space and time.
Endless songs there tell the story
of his cosmic reign sublime.

Introduction

Debbie popped into the big church in the centre of the town where she was studying. She was in search of inspiration but she wasn't looking for divine inspiration. Debbie was an undergraduate in the field of art history and her tutor had suggested she write an essay on religious symbolism. As Debbie wandered around the dark and somewhat gloomy church building she noticed that the Christian symbol of the cross was everywhere. It appeared in carved stone and wood and was embroidered on damask drapery. As she toured the building she counted more than 30 crosses. She noted that some crosses were stark and plain whilst others were elaborate. She noted, too, that some had a figure on them and some did not. Debbie knew enough about the Christian religion to know that the little man on the cross represented Jesus, but quite why he was depicted so, she could not recall.

Turning a corner into a side chapel, Debbie was startled to discover a very strange-looking cross indeed. It was illuminated by light flooding in from a rose window. It was vibrant and colourful. Unlike others she had seen that day, it bore the figure of Jesus but not semi-naked and writhing in agony, nor was he depicted dead upon the cross. Here, he was shown to be very much alive, yet still stretched out on the cross. He was fully clothed in what she recognised as religious garb and the more familiar crown of thorns had been replaced by a shiny golden crown. Debbie felt drawn to this image but could not understand why. It was quite bizarre, yet she sensed that it wanted to tell her so much. She sat before it for a while. Then she took photographs from a number of angles before she left the building and returned to college.

Researching the phenomenon of the cross, Debbie discovered that plain crosses have appealed to many Christians over the centuries because they not only remind them of the means by which Jesus was executed, but they 'speak' of his resurrection from the dead. The body of Jesus is not there! He is risen! She discovered too, that in the history of the Christian Church, many had found inspiration in crosses with the figure of Jesus upon them (crucifixes) because they reminded people of the sacrifice made by Jesus, and of how much he had suffered. However, her research revealed that Christian authorities had not always agreed on why such a sacrifice was necessary.

Debbie's research also revealed details of the kind of cross to which she had been drawn on the day of her visit to the church. She discovered that it is known as a '*Christus Rex*' or 'Christ the King'. She found out that it pre-dates crosses with the figure of Jesus on them either in agony or dead. She discovered, too, that it is rich in symbolism; that it tells much more of the story of Jesus' life, suffering, death, rising and triumphant return to heaven than does any other form of the cross.

Reflecting on her first encounter with the *Christus Rex*, Debbie sensed that it told her something more still: that it spoke to her of God's love for her.

Debbie successfully completed her essay, and on time! However, it would be a long time before she would finally explore, and reach some understanding, of what she had felt that day when she sat before that fascinating image of Christ the King.

This book offers the reader a similar journey of exploration. The iconic image of the *Christus Rex* 'spoke' to Debbie, but what might its appeal be among modern-day Christians? There will be some for whom the idea of a cross with a figure on it (naked or dressed!) will be abhorrent. There will be those who fear that praying in the presence of such an icon is dangerously close to the commandment forbidding the worship of graven images.[2] I should say, from the outset, that there is no suggestion here of worshipping anything or anyone, except the Living God! The *Christus Rex* icon is nothing more than a devotional aid. The appeal of devotional aids varies considerably across the Christian world and the *Christus Rex* is no exception.

In other ways, too, the traditional icon of the *Christus Rex* might be a challenge to some and a puzzlement to others. For example, the image of Jesus wearing vestments based on Western Catholic usage (themselves based on garments worn in biblical times) may not appeal to Christians of some traditions. In

2. Exodus 20:4, 5.

most depictions there is likely to be a crown on the head of the Christ figure but its design may range from the grossly ornate to a simple golden band. Of course, Christ had no crown on earth but a crown of thorns, which serves to highlight the fascinating paradox that is the *Christus Rex:* the Christ figure wears a golden diadem but has bare and wounded feet. His arms are outstretched, but not only as nailed there by those who crucified him, but outstretched in welcome; in expansive love. How easy it is to see the one and not the other!

In some parts of Christendom the Feast of Christ the King is celebrated on the last Sunday of October: just before the celebration of the Feast of All Saints. This suggests Christ's arrival in kingly glory just ahead of those who would follow him through the portal of death to life everlasting. In other parts of Christendom the Feast of Christ the King is celebrated just before the season of Advent: the beginning of a new liturgical year. This suggests the culmination of the story of Jesus whose celebration begins in Advent as we model how the world waited for the coming of the Saviour. However the icon is interpreted by the artist, the *Christus Rex* offers reflection on the whole of the story of what we sometimes call 'the Christ event'. Here we find association with not only his life on earth but also in terms of eternity and the bringing in of the kingdom of God. In this sense, the *Christus Rex* icon is an evangelistic and missional tool because it both proclaims the mystery of Christ and invites participation in his life.

Deeper exploration of the message of the *Christus Rex* is explored in the chapters that follow. Each chapter focuses reflection on one of a number of traditional and contemporary theological and spiritual insights as well as exploring what the icon might draw us to conclude about Christian discipleship and behaviour.

In Chapter One I explore how the *Christus Rex* offers reflection on the whole of the Christ event. The basis for this reflection is the scriptural text: 'For God so loved the world that he gave his only Son, so that everyone who believes in him may not perish but may have eternal life.'[3] This takes us to the heart of the icon, as we focus on the love of God for all.

In the following four chapters the reflection moves to three 'offices' traditionally ascribed to Jesus under the broader identity of mediator. These are the offices of prophet, priest and king. Reflecting largely on Gospel narratives concerning the life and ministry of Jesus, the reader is encouraged to consider what Christ models for us in those traditional offices and what we are called to emulate in our own discipleship.

Common to all depictions of the *Christus Rex* is the showing of the wounds of Christ, but unlike crucifixes which show Jesus with very little clothing, the *Christus* is fully clothed. Thus the fifth wound, described in John's Gospel, is not visible. Reflection in Chapter Six,

---

3. John 3:16.

therefore, focuses on Christ as wounded healer: how we bear our own wounds (apparent or hidden) and how Christ, the wounded healer, reaches out to us through one another.

Under the title of 'The Cosmic Christ', the reader is invited to consider the *Christus Rex* as an image of love which conquers all; not only here on earth but throughout all creation. This chapter is about the Church as the body of Christ. We reflect on how God, in Christ, is present among us and how his mission of love is to be fulfilled in and through us.

Material for the book includes historical research, biblical scholarship, reflections of historical and contemporary Christian spiritual writers and teachers. Occasionally, I use story to illustrate some points and to ground reflection in real-life experience. This book would be suitable for individuals but also for groups meeting regularly. At the end of each chapter there are suggestions for discussion and for prayer and a verse of a specially written hymn.

1

The Whole Story

The iconic image of the *Christus Rex* offers more of the story of our redemption than does either a plain cross or a crucifix. This many-layered devotional aid contains symbols that tell us of the role Jesus played historically and the role he continues to play.

Throughout the Christian era the Church has emphasised one or more aspects of the Christ event. Sometimes, such emphases have reflected the way that doctrine or the teaching of the Church has been influenced by particular characters or in the wake of learning, schism or reform.

Christian theology changes and evolves over the centuries as we discover more about how the Bible came to be written or in the light of experience of faith and discipleship. It changes, too, when it is challenged by life events, tragedies or conflict. The Church's teaching is challenged, too, as we learn more and more about how complex is humanity: how body, mind and spirit are so closely interwoven. What was thought to be justifiable punishment for personal inclination or lifestyle in one century is identified by the next as unacceptable prejudice or bigotry. As humanity evolves, so does theology. Perhaps it is fairer to say it does not so much evolve as revolve around the traditional truths of our faith.

Emphasis has also varied from liturgical season to liturgical season. Observing the seasons of the Church's year has been one way to apprehend something of the awesomeness of the events which began with the prophecies of the coming to earth of God in human form, in Jesus Christ our Lord. As the seasons unfold we ponder anew his birth, his life and his ministry. We go on to recollect his passion, death and resurrection, completing the annual cycle with a celebration of his return to heaven. The death and rising of Jesus is all of a piece and the seasonal liturgical celebrations of the Church's year cannot be entirely separated. Do not prayers at the heart of every Eucharistic celebration include reference to the death and rising of Christ, even at Christmas?

These events are summarised, too, in our ancient creeds. We attest to the whole story of our redemption every time we recite them so, in season and out, we cannot entirely detach ourselves with the particulars of the story without recalling its generality too.

At the heart of the story is the death and rising of Christ. The sacrificial death of Jesus has been held by Christians as the most important doctrine of faith, but that death only makes sense in the context of the doctrines of the incarnation, resurrection and ascension of our Lord. This is not to deny the significance of the cross but if we teach only the cross we do not do justice to the wonder of the whole Christ event, and we may leave those enquiring about Christianity wondering how such a happening leaves our relationship with God. To display a simple cross and to explain its meaning begs of us to place the cross in the context of God's redeeming plan. To display a cross is to display an image of a cruel instrument of torture and execution. Such an image would have sent a shiver down the spine of many people in the known world of biblical times. It would be a long time before early Christians would allow an image of the cross to have its place in churches. In parts of our world today, to display a sign of the cross as an emblem of allegiance to the Christian faith can attract derision, disdain, persecution or even death. Perhaps, however, in our culture, and over the centuries, we have so elaborated the cross, and used it in so many art and craft forms, that it has lost its power to shock.

The image of Christ on the cross, commonly called the crucifix, does not take the beholder beyond mount Calvary. We are rooted there, gazing at a figure of Christ either writhing in agony or dead upon the cross. There are, of course, times in our life when that image speaks powerfully to us because of our own experience of suffering, humiliation or vulnerability. Certainly saints of old have testified to its power. The *Christus Rex*, however, is able to offer even more. It stays true to the centrality of the Christ event and, at the heart of this truth, is the unconditional love of God for the whole of creation. The *Christus Rex* helps us to address the question in our hearts and minds as to why Christ came, lived among us and taught us.

Why he suffered and died and why he was raised from the dead, triumphant over sin and death. The answer is simple and yet profound. It is because he loves us. This awesome truth is epitomised in the words of John: 'For God so loved the world that he gave his only Son, so that everyone who believes in him may not perish but may have eternal life.'[4] It is through the lens of the knowledge of that love that we ponder the *Christus Rex*.

The wonder of the *Christus Rex* is that we can begin to ponder the love of God manifest in the Christ event from whatever catches our eye. Perhaps it is the crown or the wounded hands and feet. Perhaps it is the wood of the cross or the fine line of the robes. What might any part of this iconic image have to say to us at this time? To what is God drawing our eye?

In the iconographical tradition, wood is used as the base material on which an icon is 'written'. Wood symbolises earth; created matter. Over that the artist uses rich hues of pigment and precious metal which symbolise heaven and the divine. The icon of the *Christus Rex* is created in this same tradition. The base wood of the cross is overlaid with the glorious attire of the *Christus*. Between the layers the whole story of our redemption is told. Here I offer a five-fold schema for reflection on the whole story. This is comprised as follows:

---

4. John 3:16.

1 – the wood of the cross and the humanity of Jesus;

2 – the ministry of Jesus: arms outstretched in teaching, blessing, and bringing peace;

3 – the passion and death of Jesus: arms outstretched in crucifixion;

4 – the resurrection of Jesus who, in the *Christus Rex,* is depicted as very much alive;

5 – the glorious ascension of Jesus: The head that once was crowned with thorns is crowned with glory now!

1. The wood of the cross and the humanity of Jesus

If we ponder the wood of the cross and see only an instrument of execution we might fail to consider how significant the wood of the cross came to be for early Christians and how connections were made between the death of Jesus and his incarnation. (The wood of the manger is not without significance.) Jesus was considered to be the new 'Adam': the obedient one who restores all that is seemingly lost because humanity had been wayward and faithless. Connections were made between the tree in the Garden of Eden[5] and the 'tree' of the cross. The truth is that there could be no death on the cross without God coming amongst us in human form. The tree becomes a symbolic bridge between life and death.[6]

---

5. Genesis 2:9 and 3:24.
6. See also Revelation 2:7; 22:14 and 22:19.

2. The ministry of Jesus: arms outstretched in teaching, blessing, and bringing peace

The Gospel accounts give us the voice of Jesus as he proclaims the good news of the kingdom and as he teaches about God's love for the world and how we are to live in the light of God's love. He shows us signs of his kingdom as he heals the sick, as he blesses his disciples and as he brings them his gift of peace. As we read these accounts we can imagine him stretching out his hands as he ministers to all who would welcome him to do so. Many depictions of the *Christus Rex* show Christ with outstretched arms. His hands and feet bear the marks of the nails, but they are not fixed to the cross; rather they have triumphed over those who crucified him. Now his arms are outstretched as they were during his ministry, in a gesture of expansive love. How easy it is to see the crucified one and not the triumphant one!

John's account of the gospel was the last of the four to be written. The writer had the advantage of the early Church's reflection on the Christ event. For John, Jesus is God made human. He is both human and divine, and both identities are manifest in his ministry. For John, the crucifixion of Jesus is also his coronation. John has no problem seeing the crown of thorns of the crucified king as well as seeing, in his mind's eye, the crown of the king of heaven and earth.

The all-embracing nature of Christ is difficult for some Christians to hold. It is easier to put limitations on God's love; to believe that it depends on a certain code of human behaviour. In the history of the Church, vile and despicable things have been done by the Church in the name of God out of fear, prejudice, bigotry or discrimination. Sadly, many of these things persist, even in our so-called Western civilised society. One of the challenges of the *Christus Rex* is that those all-embracing arms are accompanied by signs and symbols of kingly authority. All authority has been given to Jesus whose just and gentle rule has begun and will never end. Sooner or later those all-embracing arms will be irresistible, and the shame of God's people offering less than all-embracing love to their neighbour will have to be overcome.

3. The passion and death of Jesus: arms outstretched in crucifixion

At the heart of our reflection on the Christ event, there is a death. It is the death of Jesus, and the significance to humankind of that death has been the subject of debate and discussion since that first Good Friday. Theological reflection on the subject is not exclusively the province of biblical writers, the early Fathers and Mothers of the Church or the likes of Augustine, Martin Luther or the great theologians of our day. Each has had something to say about how the death of Jesus put right whatever was wrong between God and man. However, every Christian can ponder the meaning of what is sometimes termed 'the atonement'. We speak of Jesus as our Saviour and we might go on to speak of being saved from sin and from eternal death. Quite how God in Christ has done that is a mystery and Christian mysteries are not necessarily to be solved (this side of heaven) but to be held. We may have come to the conclusion that there is no entirely satisfactory human understanding or articulation of it, and it is beyond the scope of this book to explore the many differing views of it. However, that does not render us any the less convinced that what we celebrate in those three solemn days between Good Friday and Easter Day has life-changing, world-changing, cosmos-changing significance. We glory in a God who so loved the world that he gave his only Son that the world might live.

Over and against that, alongside it, is the conviction that the death and rising of Christ has deep meaning for each one of us. However we theologise about it there is, at the heart of it, something life-changing about the death and rising of Christ for each of us because it is our eternal destiny. Central to our conviction is the knowledge of God's love for each and every one of us. We glory in a God who loves us unconditionally; which makes us all infinitely loveable.

There is one rationale for the death of Jesus which is not clouded in theological gobbledygook. It is that when God took on human form in Jesus Christ, he took on both human birth and human death. To have taken on human birth but then to have been, somehow, spirited away or even snatched from the jaws of death, would have meant that his experience of humanity was incomplete. He would not have been human as we are human. In modelling both birth and death he frames the experience of every creature.

4. The resurrection of Jesus who, in the *Christus Rex,* is depicted as very much alive

On a crucifix, the eyes of the figure of Christ are usually depicted as either raised to heaven in painful plea or closed in death. In the *Christus Rex* they are wide open and, quite often, penetratingly focused straight ahead. They look out upon the cosmos. They do not weep as they wept when Jesus looked upon Jerusalem.[7] The features of the *Christus* are, of course, the fruit of the imagination of the artist, but they are human features, strong and vibrant. The *Christus* is very much alive. He is the same Christ who appeared to Mary Magdalene in the garden of the resurrection on Easter morning. He is the same risen Christ who walked through locked doors and who cooked fish at a beach-side barbecue. 'Jesus is alive' we proclaim, but his 'aliveness' is unique and holds out to us the hope of resurrection for all. It holds out to us the prospect of life beyond our imagining.

5. The glorious ascension of Jesus

The resurrection of Jesus demonstrates the Father's triumph over death. In this he shows us that the same risen life is possible for us mortals. Further, in

7. Luke 19:41.

23

his ascension into heaven he takes humanity with him. The ancients who first sculpted the *Christus Rex* wanted, above all, to depict the triumph of Christ and his continuing reign over heaven and earth. Christ, as cosmic king of the universe, can seem so majestically remote from us. We remind ourselves, however, that, as Saint Teresa of Avila once put it: 'Christ has no body but yours, no hands, no feet on earth but yours. Yours are the eyes with which he looks compassion on this world.' We proclaim ourselves as the body of Christ. Through the gift of the Holy Spirit, the cosmic Christ, high and lifted up, is ever present to the world, through Christ's body, the Church. Through us, Christ exercises his authority. Where he is hailed as king is kingdom territory. It is the same kingdom as the kingdom of heaven.

This is the ultimate message of the *Christus Rex* and it is a message which demands an answer – from us! What then is our response to the God who demonstrates, in the death and rising of Christ, deep and abiding love for the world? Motivated by love and gratitude, we want to rush out and tell the Good News of God's saving love. We want to engage with the world and its needs. Our response to the actions of God in Christ our Saviour is to take action: to do something to help build God's kingdom of love here on earth. The consequences, for us, of the birth, life, death and triumphal rising of Christ are immeasurable, but we can be sure that, with the gift of new life for all, comes participation not only in the Divine Life but in the Divine Mission of love for all. This is a subject to which we shall return in the final chapter.

The image of the *Christus Rex* is multi-layered and paradoxical. It tells the whole story of the Christ event but not necessarily in chronological order. The images it contains, and the response from us that it can evoke, can be the focus of our reflection depending on our mood, on our life circumstances or on the season of the Church's year. *Christus Rex* can be gazed upon without too much of an attempt to articulate our prayers. It can be beheld as a whole, allowing us to absorb ourselves in the whole story of our redemption. The *Christus Rex* is a 'whole story' depiction because it portrays the death, resurrection and kingly coronation of Christ. It is as 'whole story' Christians that we have come before Christ, and it is as whole story Christians that Christ ministers to us and through us.

In the following chapters we explore further its messages. As we reflect upon the symbolism it contains, we learn more about the nature of Christ's continuing mission and ministry and about how our Christian vocation and discipleship are shaped by his Holy Spirit.

Pause for reflection

'For God so loved the world that he gave his only Son, so that everyone who believes in him may not perish but may have eternal life.'

(John 3:16)

Suggestions for discussion

1. What were your first impressions of the devotional aid, the *Christus Rex*? How did your opinion change as a result of reading this chapter?

2. What aspect of the Christ event attracts you most? Which aspect challenges you most?

3. Do you believe in God's unconditional love for all creation?

Suggestions for prayer

Lord Jesus Christ, King of the Universe; so far above us we cannot know you, yet so deep inside us we cannot escape you; thank you for coming among us, for being as human as we are. Thank you, that through your death and rising, you are making all things new. Help us to be your hands and your feet. Help us to look with compassion on your world, to show your love for all, in what we do and in what we say. Amen.

Lord Jesus Christ, high and lifted up, may your just and gentle rule bring peace to a troubled world. May your love for all embrace those who feel they are unloved or unlovable. Amen.

Heavenly Father, we thank you for sending your son, Jesus Christ, to show us the way to new and eternal life. Embrace in your deathless love all whom we love but see no longer. May your kingdom of love be known in all creation as it is in heaven. Amen.

Closing hymn[8]

Christ our King who reigns in glory,
yet who dwells so deep within;
draw us to your heart of mercy.
Hold us in Love's strong embrace.

---

8. To the tune of 'Come, thou long-expected Jesus' (Cross of Jesus) by Sir John Stainer.

2

Prophet to the Nations

From as early as the fourth century AD, and ascribed to the writings of the British historian and theologian Eusebius, the Church has understood Christ as having a mediatorial role between God the Father and humanity. Scholars and thinkers, throughout history, have described that role as comprising three 'offices': those of prophet, priest and king. We understand the role of Christ as prophet as being part of his role as mediator for several reasons.

First, Christ bears the authoritative message of God's unfailing love for us, even though the prophets God had sent in the past were either ignored or murdered. God has taken on human form and speaks with divine authority, validating both divine and human love. He has given us gifts of grace that will help us to grow in Christlikeness and so be able to take up our destiny of participation in the Divine Life. Scholars differ on how the role of prophet relates both to the proclamation of the Divine intention and to that of warning and judgement. However it is to work, the mediation role of Christ, as prophet, is to lead us into the kingdom, presenting us to the Father in the best possible light. This seems a far cry from the seemingly wrath-filled prophets of the Old Testament breathing fire and brimstone in the name of God. We should remember that prophets have also called for justice and mercy, and for the comforting of God's people in their time of trial.

Before we consider further the role or 'office' of Christ as prophet we might usefully reflect on the nature of prophecy as the Church understands it, and as based not only in the Old Testament but in the Gospel accounts and in the experience of the early Church.

Prophecy

Outside the Church the notion of prophecy is largely misunderstood. In the Christian tradition it is not so much about foretelling as about forth-telling. It is a way in which God speaks to us and to the world, bringing God's message of love and mercy, and guiding us into all truth. Prophecy may come in the form of great speeches, sermons, pastoral letters or encyclicals. It may come in quiet conversations with someone as the Spirit of God helps us to guide one another.

Authorities on the Old Testament scriptures suggest that prophets and prophecy are far from easy to understand but there is general agreement that a prophet is a messenger from God who speaks with the authority of God. Where it gets complicated is when one prophet denounces another as a false prophet. Whom is one to believe? How does one test the truth of prophetic utterance? Some of what is prophesied carries a caveat that the prophet's words are for an unknown future or outcome, depending on whether or not those words are heeded. Thus, the prophet might be long dead before it turns out they got it right – or wrong!

It might be less confusing if we consider prophecy in the Bible under several main headings:

Prophecies which announce

Some of the passages in Isaiah announce the coming of the Saviour – for example, Isaiah 9:6: 'For a child has been born for us, a son given to us; authority rests upon his shoulders; and he is named Wonderful Counsellor, Mighty God, Everlasting Father, Prince of Peace.' We might include here any prophetic utterances which begin with something like: 'The day is coming,' says the Lord, 'when . . .'

Prophecies which denounce

For example: 'Woe to you, O Jerusalem! How long will it be before you are made clean?'[9]

These might be distinguished from prophecies which warn, such as Malachi 2:16b: 'So take heed to yourselves and do not be faithless.' These are more like the way a parent warns a child that they will fall and hurt themselves if they persist in climbing on to the kitchen worktop. Perhaps we would say this is simply the fruit of the parent's experience and acquired wisdom, but some prophecy is just that.

9. Jeremiah 13:27b.

Prophecies which are consolatory

Here we consider prophecies which bring comfort, especially in times of difficulty or doubt. One such prophecy would be: 'For surely I know the plans I have for you, says the Lord, plans for your welfare and not for harm, to give you a future with hope.'[10] In the Old Testament scriptures there are accounts of numerous occasions when God's ancient people got themselves into difficulties or were oppressed, including the years spent in exile. One example of consolatory prophecy would be 'Comfort, O comfort my people.'[11]

The prophecies of Christ

Some of the prophetic words of Jesus may be categorised in a similar way to the tradition of the Old Testament prophets. This would not be surprising since Jesus would have been nurtured on those same ancient scriptures. Moreover, styled as a prophet, he was more likely to be heard by the people he encountered in his ministry. With the exception of his kinsman John the Baptist, it had been a while since a prophet had been heard in the land. This was, too, a people who were looking to the long-expected Messiah to rescue them. A climate prevailed in which the average Jew was subject to the minutiae of Pharisaic rules as well as to the governance of Rome. They were a people who needed

10. Jeremiah 29:11.
11. Isaiah 40:1.

hope and liberation. Many would have been keen to hear prophetic utterance in this regard.

What is distinctive and unique about the prophecies of Christ is that not only does he speak with the authority of God but he is God made man. For those with ears to hear, Christ's words are *directly* authoritative. Christ's words in the Gospel accounts include some very hard sayings: things which make us shift uncomfortably in our seats. Being open to hearing Christ's prophetic words does not necessarily mean we find them easy to understand. In that, we are no better placed than those who heard them first hand. I suggest, however, that we can pick up an overall sense of them.

It would not be possible, within the scope of this chapter, to do justice to the extent of the prophecies of Jesus. My aim is to offer an overview of them, as seen through the lens of the *Christus Rex,* which image reminds us of Christ's authority given him by the Father and to whom he accounts for his words to humanity. In this sense his words are mediatorial. Therefore, I suggest we confine our reflections to the words of Jesus in Matthew's Gospel which we have come to know as 'The Beatitudes'.[12] These bring together much of the range of Old Testament prophecy but, through them, Christ demonstrates how he has transformed these prophecies and infused them with hopefulness and confidence in God's love for us.

---

12. Matthew 5:2-12.

The Beatitudes

When Matthew set out his account of the sermon on the mount he had in mind another occasion when a mountain featured and words were delivered with authority.[13] For Matthew, Jesus is the long-awaited Messiah: he is the new Moses. In this sense he is in the tradition of the patriarchs. He is also the prophet who speaks with the authority of God. In Chapter 5 of his Gospel, the teaching of Jesus is framed in words which are so familiar to Christians: the so-called Beatitudes. Perhaps we don't consider them words of prophecy because they don't have that hard-edged articulation we are used to from some of the Old Testament prophets. They don't warn or condemn. I suggest, however, that, in their bold compassion, they are profoundly and robustly prophetic. Delivered to his audience with compassion but with quiet strength and authority, they would be enough to stir the hearts of an oppressed people. In terms of oppression, I do not mean only their subjugation to the occupying Roman army but also their subjection to the negativity of the Mosaic Law which had a tone of 'thou shalt not . . .'. The prophecy of Jesus is framed more positively in such phrases as 'they will . . .' and 'theirs is . . .'.

At the close of this chapter the reader is invited to reflect on the Beatitudes. It might be helpful, ahead of that, to ponder the relationship between prophecy and

---

13. Matthew 5–7.

teaching. Matthew records: 'When Jesus saw the crowds, he went up the mountain; and after he sat down, his disciples came to him. Then he began to speak, and he *taught* them . . .' (Matthew 5:1, 2). Christ's words are prophetic yet presented as teaching. Learning about God, and how we are to live, is learning to hear the deep motivation of God that is implied in the words. As we reflect on the Beatitudes we could ask ourselves what these words teach us about God right now. This allows that we have learned something about God from a previous encounter with the same scripture. It allows, too, that the word of God is ever fresh, new and pertinent to our faith, to our relationship with God, and to our life circumstances. We ponder scripture with a disposition of openness to hearing the authoritative voice of God speaking to our *current* need and to our awareness of the needs of the world. For example, in verse four: 'Blessed are those who mourn, for they will be comforted' might bring to mind the victims of a recent atrocity or of a scandalous dereliction of duty. But it might bring to mind, too, images of people of goodwill bringing comfort to those who have been bereaved, injured or made homeless by that same event. Both parts of that verse might inform our prayers or inspire us to take some action. Prophecy inspires action. Even prophecy which brings no condemnation or warning can bring the kind of comfort and consolation that lifts us up enough to get on with life's challenges.

Christ, as prophet, brings the ultimate authoritative voice. Through the Christ event, his voice comes not only with his divine authority but with the authority of credibility. He asks nothing of us that he has not experienced himself by taking on the fullness of humanity from birth to death.

Prophecy and the early Church

Following the events of the Day of Pentecost[14] the Church understood that Christ had fulfilled his promise to be with them forever[15] through the gift of the Holy Spirit. The gifts they had received were to be for the spreading of the good news of the kingdom, and to sustain them and build them up as they waited for Christ's glorious return. Among those gifts was the gift of prophecy. It was to be a way of hearing the authoritative voice of God, especially when the Church assembled for prayer. The long history of prophets among God's ancient people had taught them to beware of false prophets. So, Christians sought to test prophetic utterances by ensuring that there were not too many such utterances at a given time, and to discern the truth of the utterances by seeking the accord of several other Christians assembled. Nevertheless, it was not an easy matter. Some false prophecies could be easily discerned because they were in blatant conflict with the teaching of the Church. Writing on this subject

---

14. Acts 2.
15. Matthew 28:20.

elsewhere I have used this example: 'If a member of our congregation tells us that God has spoken to them and is telling the community that in order to solve their financial difficulties they should rob a bank, no one in the congregation would be able to affirm that the "word" that person had received was from God because the instruction to rob a bank would be to act against God's law.'[16]

In the history of the Church, prophecy as a gift of the Holy Spirit has been received in different ways. Some Christians have held prophecy to be authentic when it is delivered in ways similar to instances of prophecy in the Old Testament and based on the experience of the first-century Church. The prophetic words of the black activist preacher, Martin Luther King, for example, are prophetic and resonate with Old Testament prophecy, with the prophecy of Jesus and with the experience of the early Church. Prophecy takes many forms, some of which are not so obvious. Molly's story offers one such example.

Molly's story

Molly had worshipped at the same church for more than 40 years. She had been a church council member for much of that time. Molly was a reserved person; one who quietly supported the efforts of the congregation and not one to seek personal recognition. It was her

---

16. Raymond Tomkinson, *Life Shaping Spirituality: Treasures Old and New for Reflection and Growth* (Kevin Mayhew Ltd, 2014), p.73.

practice to take home the Sunday 'pew sheet' and to read again the biblical texts in the days that followed. On one occasion she had been particularly struck by a reading from Matthew's Gospel. Later that same week she attended the annual church meeting. Quite a crowd had gathered in addition to the council members.

The church treasurer congratulated the congregation on a good year of fundraising. A decade of fundraising had ended five years previously with all targets met. The church building was now in good order and fundraising efforts over the last five years had been both pleasurable and fruitful. Investments were doing well in spite of a difficult economic climate. The treasurer was thanked for his diligent and resourceful handling of the funds. The meeting was asked if there were any comments or questions for the treasurer. During his report, Molly had become more and more agitated. Her mouth was dry; her heart was beating madly. She nervously raised her hand and was invited to speak. Shaking all over, Molly asked why it was that council meeting after council meeting discussed virtually nothing else but how to raise money and how to hold on to it for the future. She said that there was never any talk of outreach, or of mission and never any support for the Church overseas or for the local community. She reminded the congregation of the previous Sunday's Gospel reading. Pew sheet in shaking hand, she read out the relevant passage: 'Do not store up for yourselves treasures on earth, where moth and rust consume and where thieves break in and steal; but store up for yourselves treasures in heaven, where neither moth nor rust consumes and where thieves do not break in and steal.'[17]

Exhausted, Molly fell back into her seat. The meeting fell silent. Eventually, the chair of the meeting thanked her for her contribution. The meeting continued and ended with drinks and snacks in the hall.

Nothing happened – at least not immediately. No one mentioned Molly's brave speech but within a year small changes came about. Collections were raised for causes other than that of the church building. The following year, a youth worker was appointed and part of the back of the church was given over to a café area to which local residents had been invited to drop in. Molly would not call herself a prophet but she spoke with the authority of God in the words of Jesus at the right time and in the right place. Much later, it would be acknowledged that God had spoken through Molly that evening, and that God's message had been heeded.

Over the centuries the Church has had to learn (sometimes painfully) that speaking up and speaking out takes courage but also wisdom in choosing what we say and how we say it. Speaking up in prophetic ways does not mean bullying people or judging them or browbeating them. It does mean speaking the truth as we understand it, but sensitively and with respect for others.

Many of Christ's prophetic words point us to the future with the establishment of his kingdom on earth

---

17. Matthew 6:19, 20.

as it is in heaven. The Church, empowered by the Holy Spirit, is Christ's prophetic voice to the world. It is called to speak out with his authority and to witness to God's message of love. It is called to show prophetic love through teaching and through action. It is called to do this even in the face of opposition or persecution. Here we recall from the Beatitudes: 'Blessed are you when people revile you and persecute you and utter all kinds of evil against you falsely on my account. Rejoice and be glad, for your reward is great in heaven, for in the same way they persecuted the prophets who were before you.'[18]

In the next chapter we consider a different aspect of prophecy. We reflect on the prophetic witness of silence and what the image of the *Christus Rex* offers in that regard. We ponder, a little, on some of those occasions when Jesus thought it wiser to remain silent than to speak out.

Pause for reflection

'Blessed are the poor in spirit, for theirs is the kingdom of heaven.
'Blessed are those who mourn, for they will be comforted.
'Blessed are the meek, for they will inherit the earth.
'Blessed are those who hunger and thirst for righteousness, for they will be filled.

---

18. Matthew 5:11, 12.

'Blessed are the merciful, for they will receive mercy.
'Blessed are the pure in heart, for they will see God.
'Blessed are the peacemakers, for they will be
called children of God.
'Blessed are those who are persecuted for
righteousness' sake, for theirs is the kingdom
of heaven.
'Blessed are you when people revile you and
persecute you and utter all kinds of evil against
you falsely on my account.
Rejoice and be glad, for your reward is great in
heaven, for in the same way they persecuted the
prophets who were before you.'[19]

Suggestions for discussion

1. Which of the Old Testament prophets inspire
   you and why?

2. How, in your own life, do you hear the
   authoritative voice of God?

3. What do the prophetic words of Jesus teach
   you about the nature of God?

Suggestions for prayer

Heavenly Father, because of your unfailing love
and your endless patience you have never forsaken
us, even though your people destroyed the prophets

---

19. Matthew 5:3-12.

you sent to guide us. We thank you for sending us your son, Jesus Christ, who told us of your love for us and of the life you offer through him. May we follow in his footsteps and speak words of love and life to others. Amen.

Lord Jesus Christ, King of the Universe, ever-living to teach and guide us, help us to listen for your voice, to hear your words in the depth of our being, that we may grow in holiness and in righteousness of life. Amen.

Holy Spirit, wisdom of God, planted deep inside us, help us to listen to one another that, together, we may discern the teaching of Christ our King from that of false prophets. Keep us from error and guide us in your eternal truth. Amen.

Closing hymn

Lord and prophet to the nations,
telling of your healing power;
show us by your death and rising,
this is now our saving hour.

3

Silent Witness

Words from the cross

The Gospel accounts of the passion and death of our Lord Jesus Christ include seven 'words' spoken by him during the three hours in which he hung on the cross. Over the centuries, these recorded interchanges with his Father, and with those around Jesus, have been a precious source of inspiration and reflection. They have been studied and commented upon by scholars and spiritual writers. Some of the 'words from the cross' are testament to Jesus' compassion and care for those crucified with him or for family and close friends who were suffering the anguish of witnessing his brutal and shameful end. As he was dying he was still caring for others. Some of his words from the cross are thought to illustrate his own anguish. He quoted Psalm 22 which begins: 'My God, my God, why have you forsaken me?' Some authorities claim this as evidence of Jesus' belief that he had been entirely abandoned by God. This, they would claim, demonstrates the final drop of out-pouring of his humanity: a requisite of a complete and necessary sacrifice for the salvation of the world. Other authorities would argue that in reciting Psalm 22 Jesus is doing what he would have done all his life: to look to the scriptures (perhaps the psalms in particular) for comfort and strength. Such authorities would remind us that Psalm 22 ends on a note of faith and confidence in God.

Gazing upon the *Christus Rex* we might note two things which are in sharp contrast to the image of Christ in agony, pouring out his heart to God. Firstly, there are no words. Everything which needed saying has been said, some of it recorded in the Gospel accounts. There are sufficient words in the Bible for us to receive the message of God's love for us, brought to us in the prophetic words and deeds of Jesus. Towards the very end of his life Jesus declared: 'It is finished.' There was no more to be said but there was more to be done. He would be raised from the dead. He, himself, had predicted it.[20] The *Christus Rex* shows Christ risen from the dead yet not disassociated from the cross, but the words from the cross, and the death of the cross, are now eclipsed in silent witness to the wonder of the resurrection.

The second thing we may note is that, whereas we might have imagined Jesus making eye-contact with the crucified thieves or with his mother and his disciple John at the foot of the cross, the eyes of the *Christus Rex* are open wide and look out. Intriguingly, it could be thought that they are looking straight at oneself; straight into one's soul. Alternatively, it could be thought that they are looking out over the cosmos; taking us all into their gaze.

In either case we are reminded of the times when Jesus spoke no words but when a look spoke volumes.

---

20. For example, in Mark 10:32-34.

One thinks, perhaps, of the encounter between Jesus and the rich young man who was anxious to do more than keep the commandments of the Mosaic law. Mark the Evangelist records that, before saying more to the young man, Jesus looked at him and loved him.[21]

There was, too, the occasion in the courtyard of the temple the night before Jesus' death. Peter had just denied, three times, that he knew Jesus. Scripture records that Jesus turned and looked at Peter.[22] How easy it is to assume that this was a look of disappointment, reproach or condemnation. How much more soul-wrenching would it have been for Peter if it was a look of compassion, of understanding and of love. It is left to John the Evangelist to make the link between that encounter between Jesus and Peter, and a post-resurrection encounter between them at a beach-side barbecue. Here, Jesus asks Peter to re-affirm his love for him – not just once but three times. Just so that we are certain to make the link between the two encounters, John is the only Evangelist to record that, on both occasions, it was a *charcoal* fire around which they were gathered. Again, actions speak louder than words. Again, we can only imagine the incisive but loving look Jesus gave Peter. As we gaze on the *Christus* we might find it difficult to catch Jesus' eye; to allow him to look upon us with compassion, understanding and love. It can be so much easier to imagine him looking at us in

---

21. Mark 10:21.
22. Luke 22:61.

disappointment, reproach or condemnation. How hard we are on ourselves! A gaze of love, and the absence of words, are things we know and experience in our own human relationships.

Both the image of the crucified Lord and that of the *Christus* show Jesus with arms outstretched. In some icons of the *Christus Rex*, however, there is a vibrancy to the outstretched arms. They seem not to be secured to the cross. The nails are gone but the wounds remain. The post-resurrection Jesus is depicted with arms outstretched in welcome, in blessing, in unconditional love. The gaze of love, the absence of words, and arms outstretched in unconditional love. These form a triad of the triumph of life over death as modelled for us in the *Christus*. Perhaps Andrew's story may illustrate how Christ continues to minister to us in that self-same triad:

Andrew's story

Following yet another row with his parents, Andrew packed a rucksack and left home. He had nowhere to go and no money. He ended up sleeping rough on the streets of Manchester. Fifteen months later, a street pastor found him delirious and incoherent. She thought he was either drunk or high on drugs. She called for an ambulance. Andrew was, in fact, suffering from pneumonia and was running a very high fever. It would be several weeks before he was well enough to be discharged from hospital. During that time, hospital social workers had located his parents who were shocked to discover that Andrew had never been more than six miles from home in the time that he had been missing. It had been a terrible experience for them and they had gone through every possible emotion.

They arrived at the hospital and were heading down one of the long corridors, when they saw Andrew, pale and thin, in a striped hospital dressing-gown, walking slowly and nervously towards them. They stood still. Andrew's mother took a sharp intake of breath and put her hands to her mouth. His father opened wide his arms. Andrew saw his father's open arms and his mother covering her mouth and felt complete and profound relief.

Following embraces there would be words – words of love and of joy. Later there would be words of reproach and words framed in questions, but the initial and essential communication of reconciliation was without words Open arms and a covered mouth would be silent witness to abiding love and forgiveness.

Falling silent

As we gaze at the silent *Christus* we might allow ourselves to fall silent too, and to evaluate the role that silence plays in our relationship with God. Do we allow ourselves to fall silent in the presence of God? Do we give God the opportunity to be heard by us? Becoming conscious of being silent is a step in the direction of a practice that has nurtured Christians' relationship with God throughout our history. Some suggest that, in our present age, there is a longing for more silence in our lives but that opportunities for it are increasingly scarce. Much has been written on how exterior silence (the absence of vocal engagement) and interior silence (a disposition of openness to listening to God) can be cultivated even in a very busy and noisy environment.[23] The suggestion here, however, is that the practice of silence can help us to choose more appropriately when it is better to keep silent and when it is better to speak out. Here we might heed the advice of Francis of Assisi who said: 'preach the gospel; use words if necessary'; or perhaps, in the words of a Ronan Keating song: 'Sometimes you say it best when you say nothing at all.'

Keeping silent and speaking out

Keeping silent and speaking out are, sometimes, a matter of judgement and of wisdom. It is a discipline, a tool which can open up amazing possibilities in prayer. It can be a comfortable accommodation of the need for space to think or to doze in the presence of God. Reflecting on the place of silence in Christian discipleship, we do well to consider how silence can also be challenging, negative, hurtful or harmful. It can be used as a weapon. In everyday human relationships silence may be used threateningly or unhelpfully. It can be strained or uncomfortable when it follows a disagreement. Sometimes silence is used as a form of

---

23. The reader might find helpful: Raymond Tomkinson, *Hard Time Praying?* (Kevin Mayhew Ltd, 2009).

manipulation. This is the silence of the person who sulks for three weeks following a row. It is the silence of the crowd that sends someone 'to Coventry' – a practice that can have very harmful consequences. There is, too, the silence of withholding praise or appreciation or of simply not answering correspondence.

We may come across, for example, the silence of cowardice that fails to speak up when it should. Perhaps we have experienced silence that allows people to draw their own conclusions on a matter whilst being pretty confident that the wrong conclusion would be reached. We may have used silence in a passive aggressive way. When I was a schoolboy it was called 'dumb insolence' and was soundly punished!

Silent suffering

There is, too, the silence that helps us to hear those who are fearful of proclaiming their faith or fearful of speaking about the fragility of it. As the people of God, we are called to speak out, to speak on behalf of the voiceless, but also to know how it feels to be voiceless and silenced.

Silence is also a kind of identification with the silent order of creation as chainsaws and bulldozers tear through rainforests, changing landscapes and disturbing wild life. It is the silence of creatures, great and small, who have no say in what happens to their natural habitat; no say in how they are abused or exploited.

We may have witnessed, or experienced for ourselves, the phenomenon of suffering in silence. This is not always a matter of stoic martyrdom. Suffering can reduce people to silence: stunned silence, bewildered silence. Sometimes words are not adequate to express grief which is the pain of loss, when silent weeping may be the only expression of it. These are times when suffering makes no sense at all and our silence merely acknowledges the mystery of it. We are reminded of the 'suffering servant' narrative in Isaiah 53 or the silence of Jesus before his accusers.[24] The psalmist suggests, 'When you are disturbed, do not sin; ponder it on your beds, and be silent.'[25] That word 'disturbed' may also be translated as 'angry'. Silence would seem to be the remedy for being disturbed or angry, yet cold seething (silent) anger can be so harmful to us. Surely it is better to find a place where we can let it all out!

Whether or not silence is a blessing or a burden may depend on many things. Those who live alone, for example, may say they get far too much silence and need to fill their day with vocal stimuli through radio or television. There is an elderly person in our neighbourhood who makes use of her free bus pass to travel on the local buses for most of the day, just so she can strike up conversations with other passengers. Silence and loneliness can be a lethal cocktail.

---

24. Matthew 27:12-14.
25. Psalm 4:4.

There is, too, the silence that neither condones nor condemns. It is the ministry of Jesus writing in the dust, as those who would stone the woman allegedly caught in the act of adultery slink away.[26] It is a powerful silence, but the corollary of this is remaining silent when something needs to be said.

We might consider silence from the perspective of someone who is profoundly deaf and whose world is silent; the human voice, the cry of a baby, the bleat of a sheep, entirely unknown. We might consider the difficulties imposed on someone who is blind when they find themselves in a totally silent environment, where silence can take away their support mechanisms, such as the warning of a hazard ahead or what the choices are for lunch.

Keeping confidences

The silence of keeping confidences can be both heartwarming and heartbreaking. Keeping confidences is not just something that clergy, healthcare professionals or lawyers do but something that is an everyday occurrence as someone shares with us something personal, something that is not meant to be common knowledge. In the silence of confidences we do not own the disclosure; we only own the silent space in which we keep them. The only one we share the confidence with is God as we bring the disclosure into our prayer,

---

26. John 8:1-11.

holding it respectfully, perhaps seeking healing, blessing, resolution, or simply sharing the joy or sorrow of it.

There are difficulties with keeping confidences. We may be inclined to break them! We may gossip! How difficult it is to tame the tongue! James, in his letter, speaks strongly about it. The following passage reminds us that problems with a loose tongue are not new!

How great a forest is set ablaze by a small fire! And the tongue is a fire. The tongue is placed among our members as a world of iniquity; it stains the whole body, sets on fire the cycle of nature, and is itself set on fire by hell. For every species of beast and bird, of reptile and sea creature, can be tamed and has been tamed by the human species, but no one can tame the tongue – a restless evil, full of deadly poison. With it we bless the Lord and Father, and with it we curse those who are made in the likeness of God. From the same mouth come blessing and cursing. My brothers and sisters, this ought not to be so. Does a spring pour forth from the same opening both fresh and brackish water? Can a fig tree, my brothers and sisters, yield olives, or a grapevine figs? No more can salt water yield fresh.

(James 3:5b-12)

Some things we hold in confidence may be an agonising burden and present us with moral dilemmas. It can be difficult, for example, if we have held a confidence of a friend, knowing that another friend has been betrayed by that person. There are issues, too, with regard to safeguarding children and vulnerable adults, or in bearing the knowledge that someone is a danger to themselves or to others. Here we rely on civil law as well as the law of God in order to be responsible citizens.

Keeping silent for the greater good?

One heartrending silence is said to have cost many lives in order to save many more. I was born in the city of Coventry just after the end of the Second World War and, as a small child, I played among the ruins of neighbouring houses which were destroyed in the many bomb raids on the city. These raids had culminated in the most devastating attack which occurred on the night of 14 November 1940. It is said that government employees, working in secret, had built a machine which could decipher enemy codes but they had to keep silent about their discovery so that the enemy would not be alerted and so change their codes. It is asserted that the then Prime Minister, Sir Winston Churchill, knew that Coventry was the intended target for bombing on that fateful night but he had to carry the burden of that knowledge for the 'greater good' of defeating the enemy on all fronts. Estimates vary as to how many people died as a result of that air-raid but some sources put the figure in excess of a thousand, although many more were injured or made homeless.

Although much has been done since the war to restore the city and to bring about a spirit of reconciliation there are still scars, both physical and metaphorical, to remind people of all that was suffered in the seemingly necessary keeping of silence.

The silenced people of God

I would like to suggest just one more purpose in the regular keeping of silence as part of Christian discipleship. It is the silence of identification with the silenced people of the world. It is the silence of the voiceless and the oppressed; the abused and the fearful. It is the silence of those afraid to speak out against evil and injustice. Keeping silent in solidarity with the silenced ones of God does two things. Firstly, it reminds us of them and their plight and, secondly, it may just move us to do something to help. Such help might be only the sending of a little money to an organisation where people are in a position to speak out on behalf of the silenced ones, or which can empower them to speak for themselves. This is silence which recalls the needs of the world but also encourages us to take action.

The silent witness of the *Christus* can give us pause for thought about the role of silence in Christian discipleship and prophetic witness. We are reminded of the wisdom of Christ who knew exactly when to speak out and when to remain silent. We have the legacy of his words as prophet to the nations, and scriptural evidence of how his silence so wonderfully complements his words.

Pause for reflection

Set a guard over my mouth, O Lord; keep watch over the door of my lips.

(Psalm 141:3)

Suggestions for discussion

1. Can you think of an occasion when actions spoke louder than words?

2. Do you have difficulties with keeping silent?

3. Are you good at keeping confidences?

Suggestions for prayer

Lord Jesus Christ, prophet to the nations, you give us voice to sing your praise but also to speak out the good news of your kingdom. Grant us the courage to bear witness to your saving love and, by your Holy Spirit, give us the words we need to speak. Amen.

Lord Jesus Christ, your word is a light to our path and a lantern to our feet. Help us to hear, too, the deep wisdom of your silences and help us to discern when it is best to say nothing. Amen.

Lord of all, I bring before you those things that have been shared with me in confidence. Help me to hold them in trust, and bathe with your healing love all those who feature in them. Amen.

Closing hymn

Gazing now o'er all creation,
silent witness to God's love.
Arms outstretched! Inclusive welcome!
Draw us all to heaven above.

4

Great High Priest

In this chapter we reflect on the second of the three sacred mediatorial offices: Christ as great high priest, ever-living to make intercession for us. Here we consider, too, what Christ models for us in regard to our own discipleship and how we respond to his prayer for the whole of creation. In particular, we consider our call to assist Christ in his ambition for peace and reconciliation in our own life and times.

Priest

Reflection on the *Christus*, in regard to the second mediatorial 'office' of Christ, is likely to be coloured by what we understand by the term 'priest'. Moreover, in many of the more ancient *Christus Rex* icons, as well as in some modern depictions, the *Christus* is wearing priestly vestments in the traditional Western Catholic usage. For this reason alone, reflection on the *Christus* regarding Christ as priest can present a real challenge to some Christians. There are exceptions to the traditional vestment image. For example, one twelfth-century depiction, which can be seen in Lucca in Italy, has Christ robed more simply, wearing a long white robe girded at the waist. Similarly, many modern versions of the risen Christ, with the cross behind him, stay faithful to the 'whole story of redemption' motif of the *Christus*

Rex, but the robes of the *Christus* are likely to be simple and more likely to have wide appeal.

In the history of the Christian Church, and in relation to ordained ministry, the concept of 'priest' has sometimes been misunderstood, held in suspicion or associated negatively with a whole range of issues. These have included the debate about whether or not women can be priests and whether there is New Testament support for the use of the word 'priest' when 'presbyter' might have more scriptural support. Some Christian traditions have opted to avoid the use of the word 'priest' altogether and have instead opted for the more generic terms of 'minister' or 'pastor'. For some, the term 'priest' is abhorrent because of a possible connotation with Old Testament Temple sacrifices.

However, much of Christendom has retained the traditional three-fold 'orders' of ordained ministry: bishop, priest and deacon. A rise in clericalism within the Church and the mysteries surrounding what a priest does at the altar, or in the confessional, not to mention the authority (divine and human) vested in the ordained priesthood, has helped to set priests apart in an unhelpful way. To make matters worse, those who have been ordained as priests have been, from time to time, put on a pedestal. Setting apart has also meant setting above! To some extent, this has also sent a message to the people of God in general that they have no part in priestly ministry.

From time to time, however, more helpful views on ordained priesthood have tended to include the notion that a priest is a representative of the wider priesthood of the Church, ordained by its members for the ministry required of them. This is linked with an overarching understanding that the priesthood of the whole Church is a participation in the high priesthood of Christ.

Given that earthly human models and forms of priesthood are a matter of continuing debate, I suggest that, for the purposes of our reflection, it might be more helpful to focus on the role of Christ as priest rather than to begin from any particular model of priesthood in ecclesiastical ministry. This will allow our reflections to transcend any narrow, limited or unhelpful connotations regarding priestliness, as we consider the priesthood of Christ, and the Church, as the whole people of God, as participants in Christ's priesthood.

The priestly function of Christ

Essentially, and religious garb notwithstanding, the *Christus* allows us to reflect on Christ as priest whose intimate prayer with the Father, through the dynamic love of the Holy Spirit, is offered endlessly for us and for the whole of creation.[27] This, as with his 'office' of prophet, is part of Christ's role as mediator and advocate. The starting point of our reflection is Christ as great high priest, ever-living to make intercession for

---

27. Romans 8:34b, though the whole of Chapter 8 is instructive here.

us. For scriptural warrant we turn to the writer of the letter to the Hebrews: 'Since, then, we have a great high priest who has passed through the heavens, Jesus, the Son of God, let us hold fast to our confession. For we do not have a high priest who is unable to sympathise with our weaknesses, but we have one who in every respect has been tested as we are, yet without sin. Let us therefore approach the throne of grace with boldness, so that we may receive mercy and find grace to help in time of need.'[28]

In order to appreciate more fully what the writer to the Hebrews is saying we need to understand a little of what 'priesthood' meant in New Testament times. Essentially, priests in the Jewish tradition offered sacrifices (burnt offerings) on behalf of those who came before them needing to pay homage to God, or to placate God whom they believed they had offended. They came out of duty to the Law of Moses, and they came also in thanksgiving for the blessings they had received at God's hand. A priest acted as intermediary. The Greeks and the Romans also had rituals in place for offering sacrifices to their gods and for much the same reasons.

The embryonic Church was wrestling with a unique concept. It was that Jesus Christ was the sacrificial victim: the lamb of God, whose sacrifice on the cross had brought about reconciliation with God. But more than that, the Church had borne witness to the

---

28. Hebrews 4:14-16.

resurrection and ascension of Jesus. They testified, too, that Christ had sent the promised Holy Spirit who filled the church membership and through whom Christ's reconciling and redeeming work could continue. This work was to be priestly in nature: Christ the intermediary between humanity and God the Father. In summary, and as awesome as it sounds, Christ was both sacrificial victim and high priest. Gone was the need for burnt offerings! What was now required of the people of God were offerings of praise and thanksgiving, and faithfulness to their vocation which was to cooperate in Christ's continuing mediatorial and intercessory role until his work of reconciliation was complete.

When one considers how long it can take the Christian Church to come to a common mind on matters of faith, doctrine or ecclesiastical roles and structures, the early Church, whose members comprised people of many nations and religious backgrounds, took very little time to grasp the mysteries of the New Covenant between God and humankind made possible by the Christ event. This is not to suggest that any of these concepts are easy to comprehend. As Christians we learn to 'hold' mysteries rather than to expect to unpack them. The mystery of the high-priestly role of Christ has enough association with historic understanding of sacrificial priesthood for us to appreciate what the early Church understood of Christ's high-priestly role. How it works exactly need not be our concern. It is perfectly legitimate, however, to ask ourselves (and one another) what might be the nature of Christ's intercessory prayer. Is it an endless list of concerns about the daily happenings of life on planet Earth? Is it like one of those 24-hour news channels on radio or television? Does Christ act as a conduit for the millions of prayer petitions that fly up to heaven every day of the week? If any of those possibilities is true then it implies two things. First, that God the Father doesn't know what's going on and needs continual 'chapter and verse' briefings. Second, it implies that God the Father needs persuading; that prayer petitions are like those petitions made to a capricious monarch at a medieval court.

The high-priestly prayer

It is beyond the scope of this book to explore, in depth, the nature of Christ's prayer for the world, but we can sense a little of it by reading Chapters 15 to 17 of John's Gospel. Scholars suggest that it can be considered in three or four parts. I suggest that it is the final part of that section of scripture which might be most helpful to our current reflection. Chapter 17 verses 1-26 are particularly instructive. This section is sometimes known as 'the farewell prayer' or 'the high-priestly prayer'. It is the longest prayer of Jesus in any of the Gospels. The way Jesus begins his prayer illustrates his total dependence on his Father in heaven. He prays for the glorious completion of the work he came to do and for those who would follow him – that is, the Church. He prays that his disciples will know the Father as he knows him; that they will be in the same intimate relationship with them both. Towards the end of the prayer Jesus prays that his followers will be protected from harm, as they carry out his mission. Supremely, he prays for their unity; not only their union with one another, but their union with himself, and with the Father. Key verses here are Chapter 17:22-26:

> 'The glory that you have given me I have given them, so that they may be one, as we are one, I in them and you in me, that they may become completely one, so that the world may know that you have sent me and have loved them even as you have loved me. Father, I desire that those also, whom you have given me, may be with me where I am, to see my glory, which you have given me because you loved me before the foundation of the world.

> 'Righteous Father, the world does not know you, but I know you; and these know that you have sent me. I made your name known to them, and I will make it known, so that the love with which you have loved me may be in them, and I in them.'

We could spend a lifetime reflecting on the high-priestly prayer of Jesus, but if we can hold in our imagination the essence of it, we can see that Christ, the eternal high priest, is making this prayer in a space and place where words are not necessary, that the vast heart of God's love beats with this prayer.

The priestly function of the people of God

Having considered a little of the nature of Christ's priestliness and the prayer at the heart of it, we come to a position which flows from that priesthood. It is defined for us by Peter: 'But you are a chosen race, a royal priesthood, a holy nation, God's own people, in order that you may proclaim the mighty acts of him who called you out of darkness into his marvellous light.'[29]

We have reflected briefly on Christ as the only mediator and advocate and on how he intercedes for us; how he presents us to the Father in the best possible light. We are his and we are to grow in holiness and in Christlikeness. This is something we do within the whole Church and not just as individuals. Christ, as head of the Church, has incorporated us: we are shareholders in the kingdom. We are a royal priesthood, a holy nation, a people set apart.

For our part, however, it is important that we understand that Christ is our great high priest, and that Christ has called his Church (the whole people of God) to participate in his priestly ministry. Central to this participation is what we understand prayer to be. I suggest that prayer is not, essentially, something we do, but a relationship in which we participate. It is aligning

29. 1 Peter 2:9.

ourselves with Christ in his mediatorial and intercessory work. As we reflect on our icon of the *Christus Rex* we notice and ponder Christ the great high priest, ever-living to make intercession for us and we join in just by holding a disposition of wanting to join in. We bring into that reflective space the people and circumstances that are on our heart. We do so knowing that, around the globe, millions of others are doing the same. Some even know they are doing it! Corporately, we are a people of prayer and being a person of prayer is what a priest is. In order to be able to be a good instrument of the gospel a priest must be a person of prayer: listening with inside 'ears' and seeing with inside 'eyes' what, and how, God wants us to be; how he wants us to live in order to inspire and encourage God's people; drawing them into his or her prayer before the throne of grace. Anyone who neglects this necessary relationship with God, fuelled by prayer, or who tries to live by their own strength and not by the grace of God, can soon lose touch with their vocation. If then, we relate that personal priestly concept to that of the whole body of the Church, we begin to appreciate what it means to inhabit Christ's priesthood. Within that priesthood comes Christ's prayer. If the high-priestly prayer from Jesus' farewell discourses does inform us of what is at the heart of Christ's prayer, we can discern what our prayer should be.

Deeply embedded in those verses from Chapter 17 of John's Gospel are aspirations for all people to belong in God, yet the Church, in every generation and in every denomination, has been quick to differentiate between those who belong and those who are outsiders. Jesus prayed that the Church, as the body of Christ, would be 'one' but the Church has fractured limbs that seem to be taking forever to heal. Far from working for reconciliation, for true 'Oneness', the Church has been slow to work for peace, sometimes waging war instead. We have been reluctant peacemakers and have not always tried hard enough to promote reconciliation between people or between nations. Jesus prayed that all would know the Father and be one in him, as he is one with the Father, but the Church is so often too preoccupied with institutional matters and the maintenance of its buildings to spare resources for letting the world in on the secret that all people are loved by God; that all are loveable.

Prayer and action

A young priest friend of mine will often say to me: 'Prayer doesn't change *God* but it can change *us*.' I understand him to mean that God does not need persuading to love us; that he doesn't need to change from the opinion he had of us since the beginning of time. Our problem is that we find the unconditional love of God for us just too awesome to believe. It is so much easier to dwell on our sinfulness than on the infinite love, mercy and grace of God! This should be enough to energise us to be more faithful, but out of love and gratitude, and not out of fear of punishment, or as an attempt to bribe our way into heaven by doing good works! As we gaze on the *Christus* we would be better sighing deeply (a prayer in itself!) and letting that sigh mean something like: 'Lord Jesus Christ, I want to grow to be more like you.' Through his death and resurrection, Christ our great high priest has changed this from a pious hope to an amazing reality. He prayed to the Father to send us the Holy Spirit to lead us into all truth.[30] This was not so much that we would *know* something we didn't know before, but that we would know God who *is* truth. It is by the grace of the Holy Spirit that we can grow in Christlikeness.

Becoming Christlike

I would like us to return briefly to the vesture of the *Christus*. Whether he wears a chasuble or not, the garment closest to the body of the *Christus* is usually a long white robe. It is, if you like, the 'foundation garment' of priestly vestments. It is called an 'alb'.[31] Some priests like to say a prayer as they put on each piece of their vestments. When the alb is put on the prayer runs something like: 'Wash me, O Lord, and cleanse my heart, that with them that have washed their robes white in the blood of the Lamb, I may eternally rejoice.'[32] It is an acknowledgement of the priest's own sinfulness but it is

---

30. John 14:26.
31. From the Latin word for white.
32. The reference to the washing of robes in the blood of the lamb comes from the Book of Revelation (The Apocalypse) 7:14.

also an aspiration of the hope to which we are all called. I like to think that I wear my white alb as a reminder to a congregation that we all belong in Christ because he has washed away our sin. At baptism, it is customary to give the newly baptised a white garment to wear. The meaning is the same. I like to think I am wearing my 'Christening robe' as a reminder to a congregation that they too 'wear' Christ.

This chapter began with a challenge not to let traditional priestly vestments get in the way of our reflection on the *Christus Rex* image of Christ. I hope the reader has seen beyond the vesture but has not discounted it. The icon of the *Christus Rex* depicts a robed Christ. Here we might draw on Paul's metaphor of how we are to 'wear' Christ in our own discipleship. He urges: 'As God's chosen ones, holy and beloved, clothe yourselves with compassion, kindness, humility, meekness, and patience. Bear with one another and, if anyone has a complaint against another, forgive each other; just as the Lord has forgiven you, so you also must forgive. Above all, clothe yourselves with love, which binds everything together in perfect harmony.'[33] Those words of Paul invite us to consider the freedom we have to choose what spiritual garments we wear, and how well we wear them. Behind the words we catch a glimpse of the society in which he lived. We know from historical accounts and from archaeological findings that people in the ancient world were as interested in

---

33. Colossians 3:12-14.

fashion as many people are today. People chose what to put on and they knew what suited them. Paul relies on that cultural understanding to make a deeper point. He uses the language of fashion as a metaphor to illustrate how we wear virtue to the point that it changes us; making us more like Christ. As we are to 'put on garments that suit God's chosen and beloved people' we might also have to divest ourselves of garments that do not suit us. We are to choose to wear garments which become us. As we grow in Christlikeness we wear spiritual garments that become *us*.[34]

Pause for reflection

Since, then, we have a great high priest who has passed through the heavens, Jesus, the Son of God, let us hold fast to our confession. For we do not have a high priest who is unable to sympathize with our weaknesses, but we have one who in every respect has been tested as we are, yet without sin. Let us therefore approach the throne of grace with boldness, so that we may receive mercy and find grace to help in time of need.[35]

Suggestions for discussion

1. Does prayer change God?

2. How has your prayer changed over the years?

---

34. The reader might find helpful a fuller reflection on this passage in Raymond Tomkinson, *Clothed in Christ: A study course for naked Christians* (Kevin Mayhew Ltd, 2008).
35. Hebrews 4:14-16.

3. In what ways does your faith community understand itself as participating in Christ's priestly ministry?

Suggestions for prayer

Heavenly Father, we praise and thank you for the victory of your Son Jesus over sin and death. Through him, receive the prayers of your people, for the fulfilment of your loving ambition for the world. Amen.

Lord Jesus Christ, great high priest, ever-living to intercede for us, may our prayers for the needs of the world accord with your own. Help your Church to participate fully in your priestly ministry, as you reconcile your people to the Father, and to one another. Amen.

Holy Spirit, you have filled your Church with gifts of grace, that we may grow to become more like Christ. Clothe us, anew, in spiritual garments that befit our calling as a holy people. Amen.

Closing hymn

Blessed Jesus, here in Spirit,
making us a holy people;
form us as a priestly nation,
bidding us to pray in you.

5
Servant King

The immediate and presenting image in the *Christus Rex* is that of kingship. But what kind of kingship is suggested here? Pontius Pilate asked Jesus, 'So you are a king?' Jesus answered, 'You say that I am a king.'[36] Pilate interrogated Jesus regarding claims that he had styled himself 'king of the Jews'. Jesus responded enigmatically and spoke of how his kingdom was not of this world. Jesus avoided falling into the trap of setting himself up as king in territory ruled over by the Romans. That alone would have sufficed to have him condemned to death, but it does not entirely account for his enigmatic responses to Pilate's questions. In a previous chapter we noted how Jesus knew when to say nothing at all. Effectively, this was one of those occasions, rendering Pilate somewhat frustrated that Jesus did not try to explain further the nature of his kingship.[37] Even if it had been appropriate or opportune for Jesus to say more on the subject, it is unlikely that Pilate would have been any the wiser. However, Pilate did pick up something that made him try harder to save Jesus from the death penalty.[38]

Pilate can be forgiven for not really understanding the nature of Jesus' kingship. Such understanding as

---

36. John 18:37.
37. John 18:33-37.
38. John 18:38-40.

he had would have been based on his own experience of kings and rulers; on how he governed and how he was subject to authority. I suggest that, in this, we have something in common with him. We, too, ask Jesus: 'So you are a king?' and we might add: 'please help us to understand the nature of your kingship'. As with priesthood in the previous chapter it can be a challenge to consider Christ as King if we begin with earthy models of kingship. We should, however, take note of how Christian monarchs, past and present, have tried to emulate the kingship of Christ.

Having lived most of my life in the second Elizabethan era in British history, I have a particular view of monarchy. It is that of a monarch who is self-sacrificing, faithful, dutiful, generous, kindly and not to be messed with! When Princess Elizabeth of the House of Windsor became 21 years of age, and while on a tour to South Africa, she gave a speech. In it she said: 'I declare, before you all, that my whole life, whether it be long or short, shall be devoted to your service, and the service of our great imperial family to which we all belong.' It was a pledge of service until death. Also during the speech she referred to a motto that had been used by some of her predecessors: 'I serve.'

Queen Elizabeth II is just one example of monarchy, and history tells us that there have been monarchs who have been overbearing, brutal and cruel as well as those who were regarded as saints. In terms of heads of state who are not monarchs one must take a global view.

Presidents of nations, too, come in various degrees of virtue and attract reputations that range from the saintly to the downright evil. It is difficult, therefore, to place the kingship of Christ amongst them, and to find similarities or contrasts. The dilemma is further compounded by cultural differences and expectations, as well as taking into account historical and political changes in how the role of a head of state is to be understood.

As we reflect on the *Christus Rex* we can be forgiven if we resist letting our gaze rest on the crown that adorns the head of the Christ figure, perhaps because it conjures up in our minds images of kingship that are both helpful and unhelpful, and which further confuse our understanding of Christ's kingship. But there it is! Our attention is drawn to that crown. In some images the crown is a simple golden diadem; sometimes it is grossly ornate and heavily bejewelled. In this, it can appear entirely incongruous, and in such sharp contrast to the cruel and mocking wreath of thorns depicted on the writhing figure of Christ on a medieval crucifix.

Someone once reminded me that 'Christ wore no crown but a crown of thorns'. It seems unlikely that Christ now wears any crown at all, except perhaps the 'crowning' of his achievements in fulfilling the Father's plan to reconcile the world. It is, in this sense, a crown with the thorns removed; no longer piercing his flesh and causing his blood to flow. It is a crown of victory in the sense that suffering and death have been overcome. It may be more helpful to think of the crown on the

Christus, essentially, as a metaphor. Perhaps that allows the mind freedom to clear away images of earthly crowned monarchs or other heads of state.

The paradox of Christ's kingship

Here we might benefit from allowing our eyes to take in the whole of the *Christus Rex* so that we see the glittering crown in context. *Christus Rex* is a king with a golden diadem but with bare and wounded feet. Here we come to the paradox of Christ's kingship. It is not to lord it over people but to be the suffering servant king.

For John the Evangelist, Jesus is already king of heaven and king of earth. From the manifestation of God in Jesus, the Word made flesh, in Chapter 1 of his Gospel account, to his coronation on the cross in Chapter 19, for John, Jesus is already, and always, king. Yet, in those poignant passages in and around the occasion of the Last Supper, we hear of the king who washes the feet of others. The parallels for us in contemporary discipleship may lie in allowing Christ to be king, and to serve through us, in all we do in his name.

Some theologians agree with John that God became man and retained his divinity along with his humanity. Others suggest that on becoming human he divested himself of his divinity. One scriptural passage in particular supports the latter position:

Let the same mind be in you that was in Christ Jesus, who, though he was in the form of God, did not regard equality with God as something to be exploited, but emptied himself, taking the form of a slave, being born in human likeness. And being found in human form, he humbled himself and became obedient to the point of death – even death on a cross.

Therefore God also highly exalted him and gave him the name that is above every name, so that at the name of Jesus every knee should bend, in heaven and on earth and under the earth, and every tongue should confess that Jesus Christ is Lord, to the glory of God the Father.[39]

As a lifelong fan of John the Evangelist, I would have to declare my support for the first theological position which stresses the incarnation or 'en-fleshing' of God in Jesus Christ. John's choice from the wealth of received narrative, and his deeper exploration of emerging Christological themes, make his position quite clear. However, the latter theological position is not without merit. Those who espouse it are grasping at something of the depth of self-abandonment that characterises God's sojourn in human flesh. Without abandonment there could be no death, and the death of Jesus was necessary to God's plan (something we reflected on in Chapter One). The scenario we explored earlier in this chapter, where Jesus engages with Pilate, suggests

---

39. Philippians 2:5-11.

something of this. Jesus does not ask to be rescued by Pilate. He abandons himself to his destiny, but we need not hold that he does so with any loss of divine indwelling, or with any degree of *lèse-majesté* on our part.

The Shepherd King

The hymn writer the Reverend Sir Henry Baker wrote a setting of Psalm 23 which still enjoys popular appeal. He chose to translate the addressee of the psalm as 'king' rather than 'lord': proclaiming: 'The king of love my shepherd is . . . !' Baker offers us a paradox of kingship which calls to mind David, the shepherd king. He brings to the notion of kingship a duty of care for the flock. In my limited experience and observation of shepherding, I learned how a shepherd has to be vigilant, caring and protecting their flock in all weathers, in season and out. Jesus described himself as 'the good shepherd': one who lays down his life for the sheep.[40] Here Jesus demonstrates the extent of his love for us. In John's theological position of the divine and royal nature of God made flesh in Jesus Christ, the sacrifice of the shepherd for the sheep is a kingly and noble act.

Turning the pyramid on its head

The paradoxical nature of the kingship of Christ turns upside down our earthbound notions of top-down pyramidal models of government. Such models

---

40. John 10:11.

are ingrained in our society and in every walk of life. Here I include the Church because, although we like to think that we have successfully inverted the pyramidal principle, that is not generally how it is experienced by many Christians in the pew.

A spiritual and temporal reign

A kingdom usually has defined territory and marked boundaries. Another way in which the kingship of Christ is different is that the kingdom of Christ, the king of love, knows no bounds. It would be a total contradiction to the meaning of love if he (or we) set bounds to it. Infinite love is just that: infinite. If any bounds are set, they are put there by us and not by God.

Another distinctive characteristic of the kingdom of Christ our King is that it is *one* kingdom. There is no distinction between the kingdom of heaven and the kingdom of earth. Christ's kingdom is a kingdom of grace, build on spiritual virtues through the gifts of the Holy Spirit.[41]

Where we find the fruit of the Spirit we find the kingdom of God.[42] For example, wherever we find the gift or fruit of love we find God. It follows that where we find God we find God's kingdom.

Christ is king of a spiritual as well as a temporal realm. By the presence of God's spirit we have a spiritual

---

41. 1 Corinthians 12–14.
42. The reader might find useful: Raymond Tomkinson, *God's Good Fruit* (Kevin Mayhew Ltd, 2002).

home and we are dwellers in the kingdom of God. Indeed Paul reminds us that we are already citizens of heaven.[43] Further, we, in ourselves, give a home to the Spirit of God. We are enfleshed spirit. God the Son dwells in us, in spirit. In this he continues to take on human form. For all of the above reasons, the kingdom of God is present reality and not just an eschatological aspiration – something to hope for at the end of time. What we do hope for is the full realisation of that kingdom, which knows no bounds and is a kingdom of heaven and of earth.

If we can identify hallmarks of the kingdom of Christ our King in the world around us, we can testify to that which is in contrast to it or in conflict with it. This includes our human experience of pain, suffering, alienation, oppression and abuse. These are the subject of reflection in the next chapter. We end this chapter by reflecting on the vessel of the kingdom of God that is the Church, and how we are to play our part in the extension of the reign of Christ the King.

By royal appointment

By allowing Christ the King to reign in our hearts and lives we not only collect a royal warrant, a kind of 'By Appointment' to do so, we also become princes and princesses in his kingdom. We are royal family. This brings not only privilege but responsibility. This ranges

---

43. Philippians 3:20.

from working with Christ in his awesome mission of love, to not bringing the kingdom into disrepute by scandalous behaviour. Our mandate comes in Peter's words to the early Church, in a passage we reflected on in the previous chapter in regard to Christ's priesthood. Reading it again, we allow the word 'royal' to colour our thinking: 'But you are a chosen race, a **royal** priesthood, a holy nation, God's own people, in order that you may proclaim the mighty acts of him who called you out of darkness into his marvellous light.'[44]

Noblesse oblige

Film footage of the coronation of Queen Elizabeth II showed the moment that the crown was placed on her head. It was the signal for the nobles of the land to place their own coronets on their head. This gesture signifies that, although the peers of the realm exercise certain ancient rights and privileges, they are subjects of the monarch. Something of this occurs to me whenever I sing the final line of the popular Charles Wesley hymn, 'Love divine, all loves excelling': 'till we cast *our* crowns before thee, lost in wonder, love and praise'. We enjoy the awesome privilege of being members of the royal household of faith, but we are subject to the highest authority in heaven and earth.

Such solemnity reminds us that, in rendering allegiance to Christ our King, we have made a solemn

---

44. 1 Peter 2:9.

undertaking; a responsibility to be carried out by all who own Christ as King of their hearts and lives. We are subjects yet he calls us friends and makes us co-heirs of the kingdom. We embrace the dignity of the state so graciously draped around our shoulders, and so gently placed on our brow. We share the glory, but also a responsibility to live up to our calling. For example, as members of the royal household, we have a duty and a privilege of care for all of creation. We are to lead the way in seeking out the lost, in clothing the naked and in feeding the poor. We note that in Jesus' powerful parable about judgement it is a king who has experienced either care or carelessness at the hands of the people.[45] This parable reminds us that we cannot assume that those of us who regard ourselves as members of the royal household of faith are the *only* ones in whom Christ dwells. Those who first heard the parable would be aghast that, as respectable and law-abiding people, they should seek out the outcast and the unclean! Yet Jesus calls on us to seek out and to feed the hungry, to clothe the naked and to stand up for the falsely imprisoned. Further, he asks us to seek his face in theirs. The embodiment of Christ in our world is not to be understood narrowly or exclusively but expansively and generously. Verses 44-46, alone, plunge Christ's point deep into our hearts:

"'Lord, when was it that we saw you hungry or thirsty or a stranger or naked or sick or in prison,

---

45. Matthew 25:31-46.

and did not take care of you?" Then he will answer them, "Truly I tell you, just as you did not do it to one of the least of these, you did not do it to me.""

Mandate of heaven

There is an ancient Chinese philosophy and belief that emperors could only continue to reign if they showed themselves as having the ability to rule, and to do so with fairness and justice. In showing such capability and wisdom, they were said to have a mandate from heaven. The people held the right to remove an emperor who failed to show suitable ability or wisdom because they would determine that the emperor had lost the mandate of heaven. Christ reigns as king of heaven and king of earth. He has given his Church a mandate to work with him for the full realisation of his loving ambition for all creation.[46] Indeed, some would go so far as to suggest that he has given that mandate to *all* people of goodwill – including, perhaps, those who are his 'other sheep that do not belong to this fold'.[47]

Christ the King reigns faultlessly. It is his Church which could so easily deserve to lose its mandate, but Christ loves us unconditionally and will never give up on us. This is no excuse for not trying to live nobly, honourably and generously in his court of Love. We have a mandate to serve. We are not slaves bound to

46. The reader might find helpful: Raymond Tomkinson, *Called to Greatness: Reflections on Vocation and Ambition in the Church* (Kevin Mayhew Ltd, 2015).
47. John 10:16.

service because we have been bought and paid for. We are bound by God's love for us; 'love so amazing it demands our life, our soul, our all'.[48] It is an irresistible draw. We cannot, ultimately, resist God because God is Love and love has to be reciprocated in order to function perfectly. We love less than perfectly but God's love, in Christ, covers all our imperfections. Paul, in his famous passage about love (1 Corinthians 13) is describing how *perfect* love behaves. It is, for example, never selfish or rude, but we know we are quite capable of being selfish and rude! Again, we rely on the grace of God at work in us, and in all the Church, to transform the paucity of our love into the glorious, and impeccable, quality of his own Love.

All God's people, as members of the royal household of faith, wear our diadems but our crown, too, has thorns in it. We feel pain. We experience sacrifice. In short, we all minister through our weakness and our vulnerability.

Christ rules!

Christ, as King, has a realm which is both heaven and earth. The significance of this is often lost on us. We may not always be aware that, as citizens of his realm, our allegiance is to our king, to his law of love, and his example of servanthood. It is a different realm from those of this earth; though Christian heads of

---

48. From the final line of Isaac Watts' hymn 'When I survey the wondrous cross' (paraphrased).

state pledge to model their reign on that of Christ. We may not often be aware that, as citizens of the heavenly kingdom, and as subjects of earthly rulers, there is always potential for conflict and we may have to make difficult choices of allegiance. In these we are not unsupported since Christ's kingship is one of grace and of his divine presence. Having returned to heaven to triumph and glory, he sent his Holy Spirit to dwell in us, his Church. Through the grace of the Holy Spirit we are given the gifts we need to live the life to which we are called. When we show in our lives the fruit of that same spirit we bear witness to his kingly power, and we demonstrate the nature of the kingdom of God. It is nothing less than a kingdom of love, joy, peace, patience, kindness, generosity, gentleness, faithfulness and self-control.[49] When we fail to demonstrate such fruit (and we all do!) we manifest behaviours and characteristics of a kingdom alien to God. We should not despair! No one is perfect, and God blesses our best efforts. Christ our servant King knows the wounds and hurts we have sustained in our many falls. He bathes and heals them. He lifts us to our feet so that we can try again.

Subject to lawful authority

We live, too, under lawful secular authority. Countries enjoying a free democracy can, through lawful processes, change those who govern them. The people can give the

---

49. Galatians 5:22, 23.

mandate to those who they believe will have the ability to govern, who are likely to do so fairly and for the good of the people. The ordering of the world in accordance with God's law has also to be achieved through lawful civil authority. In this we exercise our democratic rights and freedoms by using our vote in elections or in using our right to publicly protest. Through our participation in the making of laws (and in the rescinding of laws that are contrary to God's law), we forward the kingdom of God. In his letter to the Romans, Paul offers a very clear and comprehensive teaching on how we are to live in relation to lawful authority. He ends by exhorting the Church to the keeping of the law of love which is supremely expressed in the love of one's neighbour.[50]

So often in our reflections on the *Christus Rex* we have looked to John the Evangelist for inspiration. It seems fitting that we end this chapter by giving him the last word. As we pause for reflection, we note his proclamation of Christ:

Pause for reflection

On his robe and on his thigh he has a name inscribed, 'King of kings and Lord of lords'.[51]

Suggestions for discussion

1. What sort of obligations does membership of Christ's royal household bring you?

---

50. Romans 13:1-10.
51. Revelation 19:16.

2. What is your experience of servanthood in leadership?

3. What, for you, are the drawbacks of growing up with a monarchical image of God?

Suggestions for prayer

Christ our King, we thank you for our membership of your royal household. Help us to follow your example in servanthood, reaching out beyond the household of faith, to find you in those in need. Amen.

Christ our Shepherd King, we pray for the leaders of the Church, that they may follow your example and guide your people with love and care for all. Amen.

King of kings, guide all who lead the nations of the earth and bring all peoples under your just and gentle rule. Amen.

Closing hymn

Crown upon your blood-stained brow
shows the price of Kingly power;
marks a royal coronation:
triumph in that bitter hour.

6

Wounded Healer

Writers, poets, artists and spiritual teachers have attempted to bring us the full horror of the crucifixion of Christ but I am sure that they would admit that it is impossible to do so completely. Unless we have direct experience, we still know little of such horrors, no matter how graphically depicted. Anyone living in a society used to torture, violence, bloodshed and murder will have their own experiences, images and memories that can render graphic descriptions and depictions of pain and suffering. Anyone in pain can know what it was like for Jesus to know pain. Anyone persecuted or humiliated can know how that would have felt for Jesus. However, as one hymn writer asserts: 'We may not know, we cannot tell what pains he had to bear . . .'.[52] However, with or without devotional images and icons, the contemplation of Christ's wounds have been, for Christians in every age, a source of inspiration, fostering devotion and gratitude for all that Jesus suffered for our sake.

The reader might recall that earlier in our reflections we rejoiced that the *Christus Rex* offers us something of the whole story of the Christ event: that, unlike the medieval crucifix, this earlier depiction takes us from the horrors of Calvary to the ascension of Jesus

52. From 'There is a green hill far away', words by Mrs C. F. Alexander.

into heaven. We do not, however, leave all the horror behind. As we noted earlier, the *Christus* displays a crowned head but has bare and wounded feet. It is the wounds of Christ that we contemplate in this chapter but what might strike us immediately is that, whereas in the medieval crucifix Christ is displayed near-naked on the cross, the *Christus* is robed and offers only a limited view of Christ's wounds. Bearing in mind the way Jesus was treated as he was led to his death on the cross, his body would have borne the signs of multiple wounds. We remember he was beaten and scourged and the crown of thorns was pressed down upon his head, causing further injury. However, in the Christian tradition, we think of 'the five wounds': those in his hands and feet and the wound in his side. In regard to the wounds of Christ we come, now, to one essential difference between a medieval crucifix and a *Christus Rex*. We notice that the fifth wound, the wound in the side of Jesus, is hidden by his robes. Here we reflect on both the openness of wounds which are there for all to see, and on wounds which are hidden from sight. We reflect, too, on how Christ continues to minister to the woundedness of the world through us, even though we have wounds of our own. First, however, we consider the very nature of woundedness.

Wound care

Which of us has no experience of a wound? It could be anything from a paper cut to a surgical scar! As a student nurse I was taught 'wound care'. Moreover, I was taught not to judge the cause of a wound. Wounds, I learned and experienced, could be caused by accident, by violence or by self-harm. They could be deliberate, like those made by the surgeon's knife, or they could be accidental. They could be superficial and they could be deep and foul. They could be life-threatening or mortal. The approach to wound care was one of preventing them from getting worse or infected and of promoting healing. Here we were cautioned that a 'quick fix' healing over a wound could be very dangerous; that some wounds take a long time to heal and needed healing from the bottom up. I learned too that a wound belongs to a person, and that the story behind the wound is important; that the healing of the whole person is just as much of a concern as the wound itself. Sometimes patients would point to scars; testament to other occasions of woundedness. They might be wounds that had successfully healed. For some, those healed wounds were testament to triumph over suffering. For others, scars on their body were explications of mental or emotional scars. The pain and suffering of mental and emotional wounds that leave no physical mark can be as serious, and as life-threatening, as physical ones and also carry a mortality rate. Sometimes, because an outsider cannot see them or relate to them, they attract less sympathy, less help. The icon of the *Christus Rex* invites us to consider such hidden wounds because the fifth wound of Christ is hidden from sight by robes.

The fifth wound

John is the only Evangelist to mention the fifth wound: the one in the side of Christ. Some scholars doubt its authenticity, suggesting that (as seems to be the case in general) John is making another and deeper point. If so, then the conversation between the risen Christ and the apostle Thomas must also be a fabrication. Here I am referring to that poignant encounter when Christ appeared to his disciples for the second time. Thomas had been absent the first time and he remained incredulous at the news that Jesus had risen from the dead. Jesus invited Thomas to put his finger into the holes in his hands and to put his hand into the wound in his side. This is enough for Thomas to proclaim: 'My Lord and my God!'[53] Biblical scholarship opinion aside, the fifth wound has been a source of fascination and inspiration throughout the Christian era.

Living with woundedness

The wound in the side of Christ has been a source of inspiration because we can so easily associate ourselves with Thomas and can sense that an invitation to dwell in Christ's wounds is open to us all. The mystic Julian of Norwich wrote of her 'shewings' which were deeply inspired by Christ's passion: 'With his face full of happiness our Lord looked at his wounded side and gazed at it in joy. I followed his glance, and he led

---

53. John 20:27, 28.

my mind on from this wound, into his side. There he revealed a lovely delightful place, spacious enough for everyone who is going to be saved to rest there in peace and love.'[54] The idea of dwelling in Christ's wounds brings to mind words from the ancient hymn *Anima Christi*: 'Deep in thy wounds, Lord, hide and shelter me; so shall I never, never part from thee.'

Hidden wounds

I suggest it is important to distinguish between wounds which are hidden from sight and wounds which we *choose* to hide. The latter brings to our attention the very real human dilemma of deciding with whom we can share our less obvious wounds, the ones we either cover up or which others do not wish to hear about. Gerard tells the story of how, at the end of a church prayer and discussion meeting, he was taken aside and chided for speaking too openly about his life circumstances and challenges; his wounds. He was asked not to 'wear his heart on his sleeve'. He was told that people didn't like it and found it embarrassing. Gerard did not return to the prayer group and no one ever asked him why. He was forced to hide his wounds. It can be difficult to know when, and with whom, we can be completely open about our wounds. My experience, both as a nurse and as a priest, has taught me that people can carry the burden of a deep and painful inner wound for many,

---

54. Julian of Norwich, *Revelations of Divine Love* (Penguin Classics, 1976), p.50.

many years, choosing, at the end of their life, to lift the 'robe' on a wound which had been hidden for a long time. It can also be very hard to share something of our hidden wounds if we receive back only judgement or reproof. It can be difficult if those with whom we share our hidden wounds do not reciprocate or show us any degree of understanding. Sharing can mean taking a risk. However, many people attest to the benefit of 'talking therapy': a place to share, in confidence, those difficult to express and deeply held anxieties that can be so disabling.

Talking therapy requires the corollary of listening ministry. The value of the reciprocity of talking and listening impacted upon me when I received a picture postcard depicting the encounter between the apostle Thomas and the risen Lord. The card bore a message of thanks from someone with whom I had had a conversation the evening before. It was a kind gesture, but it was the picture on the other side of the card that had a profound and lasting effect on me, and on how I have come to understand my ministry. In the picture, Thomas is portrayed as gentle and abashed. Jesus has parted his garments and is showing the wound in his side, inviting Thomas to put his hand into it. Thomas looks as though he is placing his gentle hand in the wound. So often, in ministry, we see ourselves stretching out a strong and authoritative hand to others but seldom will we expose our own wounds; let someone find *our* woundedness, and let them gently place their hand in those wounds. The picture on the card highlighted, for me, the degree of trust to be found in deep conversations where woundedness is shared. To allow someone to stretch out their hand and to place it in the locus of our wounds is to invite a sharing of our common human condition, and to accompany one another, as we search and find, deep in those wounds, the presence of Christ, the only true healer.

There is a place, under the gentle guidance of the Holy Spirit, for a mutual sharing of our woundedness but it can mean taking a risk. The risk is that what we share may not be well received. The reaction may be one of repulsion, hostility or prejudice. On the other hand, it might be well received in sentiments of compassion, understanding and acceptance. The Dutch theologian and spiritual writer Henri Nouwen, in the subtitle of his book *The Wounded Healer*, suggests that, in our woundedness, we can become a source of life for others. In this he is suggesting that in being wounded (perhaps because we are vulnerable) we can be less resistant to the needs of others. We see this following major accidents or terrorist atrocities. People with serious wounds try to care for fellow casualties. However, Nouwen warns preachers against reference to their own woundedness in their sermons, not only because of the danger of turning the focus on the preacher and away from the message, but because it can sound like the preacher is claiming that their troubles are more profound than those of the congregation. Perhaps he is describing two diametrically opposed responses to woundedness. On the one hand, there is generosity to reach out to others we perceive as suffering more than we are. On the other, there are those whose own suffering is so overwhelming and self-absorbing that it is very difficult for them to empathise with the suffering of others.

Holding on to our wounds can also mean holding on to grudges. Some people seem better than others at letting go of grudges. 'Life's too short!' they declare. Others have allowed past woundedness to fester into deep and life-crippling bitterness and resentment. It can be difficult to know how to help them, especially if those against whom the grudge is held have died and resolution or reconciliation now seems impossible. Perhaps all we can do is to expose the wound for Christ, the only true healer, to transfigure. In the final chapter we shall reflect further on how Christ is at work still reconciling all things to the Father but also reconciling us to one another in this world and in the next.

Wounded or flawed?

Here we might consider the difference between wounds and flaws. I suggest that, in broad terms, flaws are an intrinsic part of us, whereas wounds are inflicted. However, much may depend on *how* we are flawed or, perhaps, the extent to which our flaws affect us or the people around us. Perhaps Michael's story might aid our reflection:

Michael's story

Michael, having met with his bishop, called on his spiritual adviser in some distress. He had made the appointment to meet with the bishop because he had received a letter from him, telling him that he had been rejected as a candidate to train for the priesthood. The letter said that, in the opinion of his assessors, there were 'certain flaws' in Michael's character. At the end of the half-hour meeting with the bishop, Michael was none the wiser as to the nature of the flaws or why they would render him unsuitable for ordained ministry. Perhaps the decision not to accept Michael for training for ordained ministry was based on the nature or degree of his flawed-ness. Perhaps his flaws would so undermine his ministry that he would not be able to exercise it effectively. However valid or invalid the discernment process, there was left in a heap one very disappointed and distressed person in need of support; and one who now understood himself as seriously flawed and, therefore, in his own view, of no value. His lowered self-esteem brought to mind those televised antique shows where an expert declares that a vase would be worth tens of thousands of pounds but, with a crack in it, it might sell for 50 pence at a car boot sale. We are all flawed in some way. Is not this what the writer of the Book of Genesis was trying to explain in the account of humanity's propensity to sin? However, if we allow ourselves to be defined by our flaws we will devalue ourselves. We might even lose sight of the God who loves us as we are, and as we shall be: whole, complete and priceless. Michael never did find out what flaws in him had rendered him unsuitable for ordained ministry. Subsequently, he left the Church and trained to become a counsellor. The training helped him to know himself better. His self-esteem was restored and he flourished.

Flaws are part of us, part of human nature. Some may say they are also attributable to the way we are brought up. Whatever the cause, they can become fissures, cracks, crevices and even deep ravines into which we can fall. We may need help in recovering from the effect of them. Although they are to be distinguished from wounds, I suggest that the two are not mutually exclusive. How we cope with wounds may depend upon our character or personality type. In any event, we need embracing for who we are, who we have become; shaped also by how we bore past wounding and challenged anew by current inflictions.

Flawed and wounded community

Sometimes, the very community which brings us help and support to stop our flaws becoming deep ravines into which we might fall can be the same community which wounds us or which causes us spiritual or emotional harm. One such community, which offers healing in the name of God, is the Church. When we, the Church, gather for worship or for fellowship, we come together bringing our flawed selves. We come seeking to be revalued in the light of Christ. We come not just as individuals but as a community of wounders as well as a community of the wounded; a community of exploiters as well as a community of generous self-givers. We are a community of healers but we can also be a community which can cause hurt. We are a community of flawed humanity. We are wounded healers.

Stretching out the withered arm

In Mark's account of the healing of the man with the withered arm, the power and authority of Jesus are manifest.[55] The power of his rhetoric silences his critics' challenge to his healing on the Sabbath. His power is manifest in the healing of the man with the withered arm. For the healing to take place there had to be two actions. One was that the man with the withered arm had to stretch out his arm. This may have been counter-intuitive for him, yet the authority in the voice of Jesus over-rode his natural inhibitions. The other action was that of Jesus reaching out, metaphorically and physically, to meet the need of the man. At the same time Jesus was making his major point about the Sabbath. In this healing miracle there is, between Jesus and the man, a reciprocity of stretching out. In the name of Christ, we stretch out our arm towards those in need of healing. However, we stretch out a withered arm because we, ourselves, are in need of healing. Therefore, as we heed

---

55. Mark 3:1-6.

Christ's call to stretch out our arm that he might heal through us, we remember his command is a call to trust and to believe that we too can be healed. We consider, too, that 'stretching out' implies more than a modest extension: it is a pushing to the limit, going out of our way. If we are inhibited in this, we need to ask ourselves why. For example, when we put out a hand, during the Eucharist, to exchange a sign of peace with someone, or when we stretch out our arms to embrace the Christ in one another, we risk that our open gesture will be rejected or misunderstood. If we are inhibited in this modest and somewhat scripted gesture of stretching out, how else might we be unjustifiably inhibited as we minister with the authority of Christ, which has been given to his Church, and vested in us?

We are wounded proclaimers, by word and deed, and we have the capacity and the gifting to make our wounds a place of hospitality.

Pause for reflection

He himself bore our sins in his body on the cross, so that, free from sins, we might live for righteousness; by his wounds you have been healed.[56]

Suggestions for discussion

1. Are you able to speak about your woundedness with members of your faith community?

---

56. 1 Peter 2:24.

2. With whom might you share your hidden wounds?

3. Are you a grudge-bearer?

Suggestions for prayer

Loving Lord, we thank you that, even though we are wounded and broken, you reach out to the world through us. Help us to reach out confidently to one another in forgiveness and healing. Amen.

Lord Jesus Christ, the only true healer, help your body, the Church, to bring healing to the nations of the world. Amen.

Risen Lord, we rejoice that in your wounds there is space for us all to abide, there to find grace, mercy and peace. Amen.

Closing hymn

Wounded Healer, sore afflicted,
hands and feet and more beside;
arms outstretched in loving welcome:
hide us in your piercèd side.

7

Cosmic Christ

In Chapter One we considered how, in the iconographical tradition, wood represents earth and reminds us of the wood of the manger in which the Emmanuel, the 'God-with-us', was content to rest. In terms of the image of the *Christus Rex* we noticed how the wood of the cross is overlaid by the rich hues of the robes and crown of the *Christus.* This fusion speaks to us of the union of Creator and creation: of the divine and the human. As a result of the Christ event, there is no separation between the two. There is no kingdom of heaven and kingdom of earth; but one kingdom where Christ reigns supreme. Heaven and earth are one. Paradoxically, Christ reigns but the cross still figures. Christ is risen but his wounds remain.

In Chapters Two, Three, Four and Five, we reflected on Christ's mediatorial role as prophet, priest and king. We considered how we, the Church, share in that role. We understand God's redeeming work is done but we understand, too, that the fullest expression of it is a work in progress. We recognise that we share Christ's ministry as we proclaim the Good News of God's love for us, and as we offer, with him, our prayers for the needs of the world. We know ourselves to be members together of the royal household of faith and we recognise that responsibilities come with that privilege. In Chapter Six we acknowledged the reality of our human frailty but, in humility, we rejoice that Christ is content to continue his ministry in and through us.

In this chapter we stand back from the icon so that we might, once more, see the whole story more clearly. The Christ event, from his birth to his ascension into heaven, changes everything; gives everything new meaning. It is like the way that black and white film becomes glorious colour in the movie *The Wizard of Oz*, only better! Thanks to Christ our King nothing can be the same! However, when we look about us and see that humanity is still behaving like it did before Jesus came, we wonder how it is that nothing is the same. It is a mystery: something to be gently held as we wait for understanding. Meanwhile, we live with paradox.

Scriptural accounts of the resurrection of Jesus are somewhat paradoxical. With Mary Magdalene his disciples could acclaim: 'I have seen the Lord.'[57] The risen Christ is recognisable to his followers, yet he is different. The risen Christ can walk through locked doors, appear and disappear, prepare a beachside barbecue and break bread with disciples he meets on the road to Emmaus. He can be touched (remember the invitation to Thomas[58]) yet he cannot be touched (remember his words to Mary Magdalene[59]).

The risen and ascended Christ models for us a being that is unlike anything in our human experience, yet utterly familiar. Further, he sends his Holy Spirit to

---

57. John 20:18.
58. John 20:27.
59. John 20:17.

dwell in us to enable us to become more like him, so that we, with Paul, can exclaim: 'It is no longer I who live, but it is Christ who lives in me!'[60] Thanks to the Christ event we are a new creation. He makes all things new in him. As we gaze on the triumphant *Christus,* he gazes back at us. We sense him declare: 'This too, is *your* destiny: nothing short of participation in the Divine Life.' The radical separation between God and humankind has been abolished by the Incarnate Word. I support my argument here with the epigram of St Athanasius (sometimes attributed to St Irenaeus of Lyons[61]): 'Therefore he was not man, and then became God, but he was God, and then became man, and that to deify us.'[62] This may be paraphrased as 'God became human that humans might become God'. Christopher Wordsworth put this theology of union very well in verse three of his Easter hymn:

> Christ is risen. We are risen;
> Shed upon us heavenly grace.
> Rain, and dew, and gleams of glory
> From the brightness of thy face;
> That we, with our hearts in heaven,
> Here on earth may fruitful be.
> And by angel-hands be gathered,
> And be ever, Lord, with thee.[63]

---

60. Galatians 2:20.
61. The essential scriptural warrant underpinning my assertion is: 'God is love, and those who abide in love abide in God, and God abides in them' (1 John 4:16).
62. Athanasius, *Against the Arians*, discourse 1, paragraph 39. Public domain.
63. First lines: 'Alleluia! Alleluia! Hearts to heaven and voices raise.'

By the resurrection and ascension of Jesus we are drawn into heaven to dwell, not as creatures out-with God but drawn into the very heart of God. Jesus told his followers it would be so when he said: 'And I, when I am lifted up from the earth, will draw all people to myself.'[64] Scholars suggest that Jesus refers also to being lifted up on the cross. Again the *Christus Rex* brings both phenomena together.

Participation in the Divine Life

Christ is the cosmic king reigning over all yet, far from being remote, he dwells deep in the heart of his people. Perhaps we find this idea too awesome to contemplate – at least all of the time. How, we might ask, can God dwell in humankind? The answer is simple yet profound. It is because God became human, lived our life and died our death. Now he calls us to live *his* life in God. What, we might ask, is the power by which this can happen? It is the power of love. Love is both the power of God and the very nature of God. As John asserts: 'God is love, and those who abide in love abide in God, and God abides in them.'[65] Now we make sense of Christ's commandment to love God and our neighbour.[66] We are not only to act lovingly, we are to manifest God, who is love, to the world around us. It seems easier to think of love in terms of being loving, doing loving things, but the idea of love

---

64. John 12:32.
65. 1 John 4:16.
66. Matthew 22:39; Mark 12:31; John 13:34 and 15:12.

as 'being' rather than 'doing' might be more difficult to fathom. Much depends on how we approach the subject. The mystic[67] in us will assert the 'is-ness' of the God of love who wants us to become divine. The moralist in us will be concerned with how we behave and will cite the 'doing-ness' of loving acts. As we reflect on these things we might begin with our experience of human love, asking what it teaches us about God and how we are to behave in the light of that knowledge. It is beyond the scope of this book to consider all the implications of the God-human-love relationship. Here I suggest we set aside, for now, thoughts about what one should *do* or how one should behave in order to have a loving relationship with God. Here we ponder the reality that we are as deeply embedded in God as God is in us.[68] I suggest that it is in this respect that the field of Christian mysticism has a contribution to make. It engages with both the phenomenon and the process of the divination of all creation: the divine dwelling of God in humankind (in Jesus Christ) being held as the *de facto* consequence of the Christ event.

We reflected earlier on the reference by John to the wound in the side of the dead Jesus.[69] He records that, once pierced by the soldier's lance, blood and water came pouring out. Those intent on a rational explanation of this are puzzled that anything would flow *post-mortem*

---

67. I am using the term 'mystic' to mean anyone who is aware of God within them and all around them.
68. 1 John 4:16.
69. John 19:34.

but also by what physiological phenomenon this might happen. Those used to John's layer upon layer of theological reflection might be content to understand him to be referring to the fusion of the divine (the royal blood) with creation (water). There is a prayer which some priests like to say when, during a Eucharistic celebration, they add a little water to the wine in the chalice. It runs something like: 'By the mystery of this water and wine, may we come to share in the divinity of Christ, who humbled himself to share in our humanity.'

We are called to love. We are called to serve, but we are also called to participate in the Divine Life which is a dynamic love. Our transformation into the Divine Life is a process of becoming ultimately real. As John points out: 'We love because he [God] first loved us.'[70] Love is God's nature and God's initiative. Our response to God is rooted in our desire to love God back, which is our core vocation. This reciprocation of loving, and being loved, is the dynamic of our life in God. Moreover, we are called to evidence God (who is Love) in our own loving, no matter how imperfect that loving is. Evidencing love in our lives demonstrates that God is present in us. Growth in love is growth in 'divination' (transformation towards becoming divine) which is something to which the whole of creation is called.

Christ's body the Church

The living body of Christ, the Church here on earth and in heaven, is a royal body in which we share. Here on

---

70. 1 John 4:19.

earth it is a wounded majestic body, as well as a glorious body. It is called to be a 'place' of hospitality. We don't often make the connection between woundedness and hospitality except in terms of 'hospital'. Both words come from the same Latin root: *hospes*, meaning 'guests'. We are called to stretch out our wounded and withered arms in hospitable invitation. Extension of the kingdom of God is an extension of God's unconditional love. If we place limits on that love, we inhibit the kingdom. God's love is demonstrated in expansive welcome. However, a survey of church communities would show us that there are degrees of welcome extended; degrees of hospitality demonstrated in those church communities and congregations. For example, at the Last Supper, Jesus prayed for the unity of the Church, but we find that Eucharistic hospitality (Holy Communion) is not extended by some Christians to others. A survey would show that some churches promote themselves as 'inclusive' but this can mean simply the provision of large-print books for people with sight difficulties, or the installation of a ramp to allow easier access for a wheelchair. Inclusivity policies and practice may not extend to a welcome for people who are gay, unkempt, disruptive or of certain ethnic backgrounds.

When we think of Christ's wounds we might think of those saints in our history who have borne similar marks in their hands and feet. We call this 'stigmata', which is the plural of the word 'stigma', meaning a mark or wound on the body. But the word stigma (or stigmatisation) is used also to mean the 'branding' of someone in disgrace for some personal characteristic, quality, action or circumstance.[71] Whenever and wherever we set limits on whom we are prepared to welcome in the name of God, we stigmatise those people. As we reflected earlier, Jesus' remark about being lifted up is likely to refer both to his crucifixion and to his lifting up, in glory, as king of heaven and king of earth. It is also a pledge that he will draw all people to himself. He draws *all* people and it is not up to us to decide, on his behalf, which people are good enough or orthodox enough to be drawn by him. In his pledge, Jesus does not single out anyone as being beyond his divine drawing. The cosmic Christ, through his body the Church, continues to draw all people into a relationship with him.

Christ's mission is our mission

Issues of the Church as an institution are coloured by what is understood to be its purpose under God. As there has been no consistent and commonly held understanding of it, reflection and teaching have sometimes led to division and to schism. This has sometimes laid the Church open to fashion and fad. More constructively, it has afforded opportunities for pastoral response to social change and to the influence of secular disciplines such as the social sciences. The Church no longer imprisons

---

71. Shorter Oxford English Dictionary, p.3027.

scientists who argue that the world is round but, sometimes, it does still condemn those whose faith identity does not fit its own paradigm. Moreover, confusion as to God's ambition for the world can lead to self-serving ambition purporting to be God's will. This can lead to destructive narcissistic behaviour.[72] Seeking an understanding of God's purpose is central to the exploration of vocation but it can be difficult to discern whose will is being served. The Church is called to embody Christ, to reach out in his name in making God's infinite love known in all the world. God's love is unconditional and Christ's body cannot offer less. The mystic in us unites with the moralist in us. Knowing of love, and responding lovingly to the love of God in how we behave, is the true foundation of moral theology. By our baptism into the death and rising of Christ we carry the light of Christ within us: we take that light into the night-time places of unbelief and ignorance; the night-time lives of suffering and affliction; and the dark-night places of spiritual and physical death. But this light we carry is made the brighter because we do not carry it alone: we walk in the light of Christ and we walk together. Together we are the resurrection body of Christ, bringing his light to the night-time places of this world.

As we rejoice in who we are in Christ, we ever seek to do what Jesus Christ did on earth and continues to

72. A fuller discussion of this may be found in Raymond Tomkinson, *Called to Greatness: Vocation and Ambition in the Church*.

do until all creation participates in the Divine Life. Christ our King knows what he asks of us, and by the grace of the Holy Spirit ensures we have all we need for the fulfilment of God's ambitious love.

Pause for reflection

We love because he [God] first loved us.[73]

Suggestions for discussion

1. When are you most aware of God's presence in you and around you?

2. Is your faith community truly 'inclusive'? If not, how could it be more welcoming?

3. How do you participate in Christ's mission of love for all?

Suggestions for prayer

Christ our King, you are high and lifted up in majesty, yet you dwell deep within us. As we hold this mystery, help us to recognise your presence in us and in the world around us. Amen.

Christ our King, ever-living to draw all to yourself, forgive us the scandal of our prejudices and the bounds we set in your name. Amen.

---

73. 1 John 4:19.

Christ our King, help your body, the Church, to witness to your saving love in both word and deed, until the fulfilment of your loving ambition for all creation. Amen.

Closing hymn

Christ our King now reigns in glory
o'er all worlds in space and time.
Endless songs there tell the story
of his cosmic reign sublime.

Further reading

Athanasius, *Against the Arians*, discourse 1, paragraph 39. Public domain.

Julian of Norwich, *Revelations of Divine Love* (Penguin Classics, 1976).

Tomkinson, Raymond, *Called to Greatness: Vocation and Ambition in the Church* (Kevin Mayhew Ltd, 2015).

Tomkinson, Raymond, *Life Shaping Spirituality: Treasures Old and New for Reflection and Growth* (Kevin Mayhew Ltd, 2014).

Tomkinson, Raymond, *Called to Love: Discernment, Decision Making and Ministry* (SCM Press, 2012).

Tomkinson, Raymond, *Hard Time Praying?* (Kevin Mayhew Ltd, 2009).

Tomkinson, Raymond, *God's Good Fruit* (Kevin Mayhew Ltd, 2002).